CREDIT UNION POLITICAL ACTION HANDBOOK

Produced by the Center for Professional Development
CUNA & Affiliates
Madison, Wisconsin

Product #21305

Cover:
Flag image © 1998 PhotoDisc, Inc. Capitol building courtesy of Corel.

This publication is designed to provide accurate and authoritative information in regard to the subject matter covered. It is sold with the understanding that the publisher, Credit Union National Association, Inc., is not engaged in rendering legal, accounting, or other professional services. If legal advice or other expert assistance is required, the services of a competent professional person should be sought.

Written by Steven Patrick Rodeman and Scott Spoolman
Produced by Jim Jerving and Jeremiah Cahill
Production assistance by Elaine Harrop

Copyright © 1998 by Credit Union National Association, Inc.

ISBN 0-7872-5056-2

All rights reserved. No part of this publication may be reproduced, stored in a retrieval system, or transmitted, in any form or by any means, electronic, mechanical, photocopying, recording, or otherwise, without the prior written permission of the copyright owner.

Printed in the United States of America
10   9   8   7   6   5   4   3   2   1

CONTENTS

Acknowledgments v
About the Authors v
Introduction vii

CHAPTER ONE: OVERVIEW OF THE POLITICAL PROCESS 1
    Components of Government 1
    Legislative Process 8
    Elections 9
    Proportional Representation 11

CHAPTER TWO: CREDIT UNIONS AND POLITICS 13
    Origins of Credit Unions through Politics 13
    Role of Credit Unions as Cooperatives in Politics 16
    History and Evolution of Credit Union Political Action 18
    Credit Unions' Political/Legislative Framework 21
    Role of Credit Union Leagues/CUNA 22

CHAPTER THREE: ELECTIONS 25
    Political Parties and Candidates 25
    The Campaign 28
    Introduction to Political Action Committees 34

CHAPTER FOUR: THE LEGISLATIVE PROCESS 39
    How a Bill Becomes a Law 39
    Opportunities for Input 43
    Relationship between Elections and Lawmaking 54

CHAPTER FIVE: CREDIT UNIONS IN THE ELECTION PROCESS 57
    Importance of Relationship Building 57
    Political Contributions 62
    Credit Union PACs in the Election Process 66
    In-Kind Contributions 70
    Chapter/Annual Meetings 71
    Member Education/Partisan Communications 72

CHAPTER SIX: CREDIT UNIONS IN THE LEGISLATIVE PROCESS **75**
    Learning the Rules of the Legislative Game   76
    Use of Outside Legislative Counsel   80
    Legislative Staff   82
    Lobbying Basics   83

**CHAPTER SEVEN: CREATING A POLITICAL CULTURE
                    IN YOUR CREDIT UNION** **93**
    Mission Statement or Vision   93
    Board Responsibility and Commitment   94
    Staff and Professionals' Commitment   95
    Integrating Political Action into Your Corporate Culture   100

APPENDIX: NCUA DOCUMENTS **103**

BIBLIOGRAPHY **111**

ACKNOWLEDGMENTS

This handbook benefited from the comments of several credit union professionals. We wish to thank the following people for their helpful reviews: Susan M. Bushnik, Hamilton Standard Federal Credit Union, Windsor Locks, Connecticut; Cindy Connelly, Georgia Credit Union Affiliates; Larry Hanna and Michael Reisnour, First Community Credit Union, Jamestown, North Dakota; Patrick Jury, Iowa Credit Union League; Christina Moraski, WCTA Federal Credit Union, Sodus, New York; and Rick Wargo, Pennsylvania Credit Union League. Also, Carol Austin, Jeremiah Cahill, Elaine Harrop, Rachel Imsland, and Jim Jerving of CUNA & Affiliates provided invaluable support.

ABOUT THE AUTHORS

Steven Patrick Rodeman is general counsel with Safeway Northwest Central Credit Union. His areas of responsibility include compliance and collection policies, as well as providing assistance regarding legal aspects of the credit union's lending and operations. Previously, he spent over ten years with the Oregon Credit Union League, serving five of those years as vice-president of legislative and regulatory affairs. He was responsible for the league's dues-supported activities, including governmental affairs and lobbying of federal, state, and local legislative bodies. In addition, he was named general counsel for the league and its affiliated organizations.

Rodeman lectures frequently on several aspects of financial institution and credit union laws and regulations. He has spoken at credit union league and attorney conferences all around the country. He is the author of *A Director's Guide to Credit Union Regulations and Exams,* published by CUNA's Center for Professional Development. He also contributes to CUNA's *Directors Newsletter* on compliance and policy issues for credit union volunteers, and to the *Managing Y2K* newsletter on legal issues pertaining to the millennium bug.

Scott Spoolman is a professional writer and editor who has contributed to *Credit Union Magazine* as a feature writer. After getting a master's degree in journalism, he spent nine years in the publishing industry managing the development and publication of college textbooks, including several texts in the field of politics and government. He runs his own writing and editorial services business.

INTRODUCTION

Credit unions have gained respect and grown in popularity, but their right to exist is far from guaranteed. They were established through the passage of laws, and in the same way, they can be eliminated. Every year, laws that determine the future of credit unions are made through political processes at all levels of government—local, state, and federal. If credit unions are to thrive, or even to survive as a viable part of the financial marketplace, credit union management, employees, volunteers, and members need to take an active role in those political processes.

The credit union movement has long held a tradition of neutrality in the political world. This principle stemmed from the need for credit unions to be available to all people, regardless of their political leanings. The spirit of cooperative ownership so crucial to the movement tends to make us shy away from taking positions on political issues that might make some of our members feel alienated and excluded.

Our attitude of neutrality in politics must take a backseat when we are faced with issues that are vital to the health and well-being of credit unions. On these issues, there is no choice but to take a side. We must break out of old habits, and take on challenges that are new to many of us. We all have a clear mission and responsibility in the political process, and that is to guarantee the continued existence of credit unions.

While it may seem like exaggeration, nothing less than the continued existence of the credit union movement is at stake in today's political game. The banking industry is aggressively campaigning to remove credit unions from competition, or to force them to remold themselves into the bankers' image. That effort has taken the form of lobbying, political contributions, and public relations campaigns. In fact, banks currently outspend credit unions by more than twelve-to-one on political contributions and four-to-one on professional lobbying activities. Clearly, banks are taking sides in the political arena.

The credit union movement certainly can claim political successes. But while we have scored some major goals, the game is far from over. Challenges in the political arena will continue. To be politically active in our own interest is now a higher priority for anyone who values credit unions.

Those people whose contact with credit unions is limited may have a hard time realizing how important we are to our members. They may be unaware of how much good work credit unions do every day. Many legislators fall into this category. They need more information on the work we do, and on how crucial it is for consumers to have a choice of financial services providers. And who better to provide them with regular reminders than those of us who are immersed in the credit union movement every day? We, who know how much we improve our members' lives and financial well-being, need to be the messengers. And the more voices carrying the message, the more clearly it will be heard.

CHAPTER ONE

OVERVIEW OF THE POLITICAL PROCESS

We often speak of politics as if it were a game. Political news coverage typically includes references to rules, penalties, playing fields, winners, and losers. To be an effective player—to win at the game of politics—you need to know who the players are, and how and where the game is played.

> *To win at the game of politics—you need to know who the players are, and how and where the game is played.*

COMPONENTS OF GOVERNMENT

Each level of government could be considered an arena in which the game of politics is played. We will start with the biggest arena of all—the federal government. As we learned in grade-school civics classes, it has three major branches: the legislative branch, the executive branch, and the judiciary. Each of them takes a major role in the political processes described in this handbook.

The Legislative Branch

At the heart of the federal government is the Congress, which makes the laws by which we live. Established in the first article of the Constitution, it was considered by many of the founders to be the most important of the governmental units. In addition to its legislative powers, it also has the power to supervise agencies created by law, to oversee how laws are being enforced, and to investigate matters of law at the highest levels of government.

The country's founders believed in a **bicameral,** or two-chamber, legislature like the English Parliament of their time. They wanted to disperse power—to prevent one branch of government from dominating all others. They envisioned two chambers—each with roughly equal legislative powers, each serving as a check on the other.

The two houses—the House of Representatives and the Senate—differ in many ways. The House of Representatives (or simply the House) in some ways is closer to the people and more sensitive to their opinions. There are 435 representatives and 100 senators, so most of the representatives represent smaller geographic areas and fewer people than the senators in their states do. The exceptions are the fourteen states with only one or two representatives each. Representatives serve two-year terms. In the political world, two years pass quickly, especially with the advent of more aggressive and expensive election campaigns. So representatives spend both of those years being very attentive to their reelection prospects. This means they need to spend much of their time attending to what the voters and interest groups tell them.

The Senate, on the other hand, has two people from each state, regardless of the state's size. Senators serve six-year terms and so have a few more years per term in which to put the reelection campaign on the back burner. You must wait until your thirtieth birthday to serve in the Senate, whereas in the House you need be only twenty-five years old. The founders apparently wanted the Senate to be a slightly more mature body, and perhaps more sedate and deliberative, and more removed than the House is from the stormy seas of public opinion.

Both houses employ committees and subcommittees to get their work done. Congress, whether or not you consider it to be productive, has a tremendous amount of work to do, so that work is divided up among the members. Almost every single bill introduced in Congress gets assigned immediately to one of the many **standing committees,** each of which is dedicated to one large policy area such as agriculture or banking. Most bills never get beyond this stage. Instead of being processed by the committees and referred back to the House or Senate floor for debate, most bills are set aside and die in committees. Clearly, the committees are important centers of power within government.

Here is an important area where the House and Senate are different. House committees have more members than Senate committees, but representatives tend to serve on fewer committees than do senators. Representatives become specialists on their committees, while senators attend to more issues and become generalists. The specialists sometimes get a lot of attention from colleagues, lobbyists, and others who want their help. Also, seniority usually determines who becomes chair of a committee, which is a powerful position. The chair and the chair's allies have a lot to say about how bills are handled in committee. It pays for those who want to be politically active to know who the specialists and other key players are—to know as much as possible about all the committee members dealing with their issues.

Another aspect of Congress that grows more important every year is the **congressional staff.** As our society, our economy, and our laws become larger and more complex, senators and representatives have more and more work to do. They hire people to help them stay on top of the issues and all the legislation that is introduced. They rely on their staffs increasingly to keep them informed, so that they can influence as much legislation as possible. On many issues, key staff people working for powerful members of Congress can play a central role in policy making. Citizens and groups seeking to influence the process would do well to know who those key staffers are.

The Executive Branch

The second branch established by the Constitution is the executive branch. Today, this means the president, the president's staff, and the enormous federal bureaucracy. The president's position is intended to be powerful, based on the Constitution, on laws passed, and on precedents set by executives over the years. But as with the other two branches, the executive's power is also limited by design. For example, while Congress determines how much money is spent and where, most spending laws give the president limited power to redirect funds according to certain guidelines. Yet, the federal courts can rule a president's actions unconstitutional. And the president can nominate people to sit as federal judges, but those appointments must be approved by the Senate.

Most of us never talk with or deal directly with the president of the United States. But all of us deal with the executive branch in one way or another through the federal bureaucracy. From the Department of Agriculture to the IRS to the U.S. Postal Service, this conglomeration of regulatory agencies, government corporations, and cabinet departments does the day-to-day work of the government.

When Congress and the president pass a law, they have generated something comparable to a design sketch for a new automobile. Agencies like the National Credit Union Administration (NCUA) then make detailed regulations that are akin to the detailed working drawings for the new machine based on the design sketch. They then oversee the building of the machine and monitor its functions.

They are also charged with making sure the machine runs as intended and with making adjustments to the rules, as necessary, to accomplish that purpose.

Another important function of the bureaucracy is adjudication of its rules. The executive branch employs nearly thirteen hundred **administrative law judges,** who hear and rule on disputes between parties over the federal regulations. It is interesting that these judges are appointed and cannot be fired except for gross misconduct. In recent years, as federal agencies have gained more power in regulating economic activity, these judges have become more powerful.

Another aspect of the bureaucracy worth noting is an arrangement labeled by political scientists as an **iron triangle.** The three sides of the triangle represent a congressional committee, a regulatory agency, and an interest group, all working on the same issue. The three-way relationship grows stronger, and sometimes becomes detrimental to the legislative process, when the three sides act to further their own interests and to strengthen each other mutually. For example, an interest group might help committee members by employing lobbyists to provide research, information, and assistance with drafting legislation. That legislation might in turn support the agency by helping it to get the budget resources it requires to keep its programs alive and well. In the worst case, the agency gives preference to the interest group in making and enforcing its rules. And the interest group keeps the cycle going by funding more assistance to the congressional committee.

These arrangements, while they sometimes benefit the nation as a whole, tend to narrow the focus of legislation and regulation. As a result the interests served tend to be those of the interest group involved more than the interests of the public. For those who want to influence the political process, it is a good idea to learn how and where the iron triangles operate.

The Judiciary

The federal court system has evolved considerably since it was established within the Constitution to be the third of three equally powerful branches of government. The founders left it to Congress to decide exactly how the judiciary should be structured. Congress passed a law to create the Supreme Court with its chief justice and eight associate justices. All justices are to be appointed by the president with the advice and approval of the Senate. Unless they choose to resign or are impeached by Congress, the justices can serve throughout their lives.

Congress also established the federal **district courts,** of which there are now eighty-nine, where most federal cases begin and end. Depending on how much work there is to do within the districts, these courts have from two to twenty-eight judges. In total, there are 610 federal district judges. It's been said that we live in a litigious society, and statistics bear that out. The number of civil cases entered in federal district courts has increased from 87,300 in 1970 to over 272,000 in 1996. The number of cases reaching trial, however, stays relatively steady at between 8,000 and 10,000 per year.

A little over a hundred years ago, Congress saw the need for appeals courts to assist the Supreme Court with its increasing caseload. There are now thirteen courts of appeals, which hear most of the appeals of decisions made by federal courts and administrative agencies. Each state and territory is assigned to one of eleven **circuits,** or geographic areas. The District of Columbia has its own circuit. And the thirteenth court, the Court of Appeals for the Federal Circuit, specializes in patent cases, international trade cases, and some civil cases in which the U.S. government is a defendant.

As district court and administrative agency rulings are appealed to the courts of appeals, their decisions are to be final, except when the law provides for direct review of the cases by the Supreme Court. The Supreme Court can choose whether or not to hear cases appealed to it from the courts of appeals, and most cases are declined by the Supreme Court. Supreme Court rulings are final, unless Congress and the president pass new laws or propose constitutional amendments to overturn them. An obvious example of this sort of process is the credit union field of membership case.

The federal courts were originally designed not to be players in the game of politics. They were supposed to be more like the referees, applying the rules but not changing them in any way. The Supreme Court, however, established two key powers early in its life—the power to overturn the rulings of state courts and the power of **judicial review.** The latter has made all federal courts players in the game, because with judicial review, they can declare actions of the president and Congress unconstitutional, thus nullifying them. Hence, courts can play an active role in policy making.

Some observers say that the power of judicial review has been abused by **judicial activists**—judges who want to have a strong hand in policy making. Most people find judicial activism to be unacceptable, but that judgment is a subjective one. In times when courts have handed down liberal decisions, conservatives have accused them of judicial activism. Liberals make that accusation when they consider court decisions to be conservative. Regardless of where on the spectrum the decisions land, it is clear that courts have become powerful in the policy-making arena. Key court decisions have affected all of our lives on matters such as prayer in public schools, environmental regulation, and, of course, credit union fields of membership.

Key court decisions have affected all of our lives.

State Governments and How They Work with the Federal Government

While the fifty state governments vary considerably, they strongly echo the federal government in their design and function. All the states have the same three branches of government as the federal government has, and they tend to employ checks and balances in a similar way. Each state has a constitution. Again, they echo the U.S. Constitution in their structure, although they tend to be much more detailed and they change more often. The state legislatures vary greatly in size and makeup. All except Nebraska's one-house legislature use the bicameral model. Governors of the various states have powers that are similar to, as well as powers that are different from, those of the president.

The game of politics is played no less vigorously in the states. As President Reagan and the Republican-led Congress have sought to return more decision-making power and more money to the states, lobbyists have flocked to the state houses. In turn, the states in general have regulated lobbying more strictly than does the federal government. Most states require lobbyists to register, to identify their employers, and to report their business expenditures.

To some extent, government is more direct at the state level than at the federal level. That is, voters in most states have more power to affect changes in state government. Mechanisms like **referenda** and **initiatives** allow citizens to make changes in the law by directly voting on them. Also, voters in many states can strongly affect the processes of government through **recall votes,** which can end the terms of elected officials before their time is up. At least, the threat of a recall vote gives citizens and interest groups some extra leverage.

The story of the evolving relationship between the state and federal governments is long and complicated. The framers of the Constitution agreed upon a system whereby the two levels would share power. The federal government would have the power to maintain order. But it was restricted in its power to influence individual freedoms and the freedom of the states to govern themselves. The Supreme Court extended federal power by holding that states are governed by the U.S. Constitution.

This system of **federalism** became the foundation on which a complicated structure of laws and relationships has developed. The balance of power has changed over the years, with federal power growing and diminishing. It has been a process so dramatic and dynamic that it involved even a civil war. But essentially, the concept of shared power—based on rule of law, separation of powers, and the Bill of Rights—has prevailed.

The concept of shared power—based on rule of law, separation of powers, and the Bill of Rights—has prevailed.

Probably the most significant change in the federal-state relationship resulted from the New Deal programs of the 1930s. That was when federal financial assistance to states became a huge and integral part of the system of federalism. Over the years, states became dependent on a tremendous flow of federal money for funding their programs. The federal government, by granting or withholding its money, was able to use it as a tool for accomplishing its goals, and its power over the states increased where money was an issue.

Since the presidency of Ronald Reagan, there have been consistent efforts to decrease this fiscal relationship and to make the states less dependent on, and less subject to, federal money and power. While this gives the states a harder time in funding their programs, it also gives them more power in the outcomes of those programs. Although the share of state budgets supported by federal money has declined since Reagan was president, federal aid remains a major source of state revenue.

The federal-state relationship will continue to evolve and power will continue to shift as events and circumstances play out. But the question of how the power is distributed and how it is shifting at any given time is a key question for each and every player in the political arena.

LEGISLATIVE PROCESS

At the core of our government is the lawmaking process. It is at the center of the political game. Each year in the U.S. Congress, the process begins early in January with the swearing in of new members, and later in that month, the legislative session begins. Typically, it runs until some time in October, with periodic recesses of a week or more. Most representatives and senators, on any given day of a session, are busy with floor debates, committee hearings, and staff and committee meetings.

States legislatures, of course, vary in how often and how long they meet to conduct the business of lawmaking. Usually, the floor sessions are shorter than those of the U.S. Congress. A typical state legislature has floor sessions during most weeks of January through March, a veto review period in April, and committee work scheduled during the rest of the year, with special sessions called occasionally for various reasons.

In Congress, and in most state legislatures, the process of passing a law is roughly as follows:

1. A **bill** proposing new legislation is introduced by a legislator in either house.
2. The bill is considered by a committee and usually referred to a subcommittee.
3. In subcommittee, it may simply be set aside. If not, hearings may be held, and the bill might possibly be amended and then reported back out to the full committee.
4. The full committee might or might not subject the bill to the same process. Eventually, if the majority of the committee supports it, it is brought to the floor of the house in which it started, for debate.
5. If it gains the support of a majority of that house, the bill is passed to the other house, where the process begins again.
6. If the bill passes both houses, it is sent to the executive to be signed or vetoed.
7. If it is signed, it becomes law; if vetoed, the legislators have an opportunity to override the veto; if two-thirds or more of the legislature vote again for the bill, it becomes law, despite the veto.

We explore the process of lawmaking much more fully in chapter 4. We also examine how and when citizens and interest groups can influence that process by means such as lobbying, using political action committees, and working at the grassroots level. In chapter 6, we look at how to apply all of this for the benefit of credit unions. We consider how to build relationships with government representatives and how to make the most of our efforts at influencing legislation and regulatory processes.

Another fundamental element of the political game that strongly affects lawmaking is the election process. Like other elements of the game, the story of elections is long and complicated. We introduce it here and cover it more elaborately in chapter 3.

ELECTIONS

General elections for federal offices are held the first Tuesday following the first Monday in November of every even-numbered year. With each election, the entire House and one-third of the senators stand to lose their seats or to be elected for another term. As we all know, the presidential election is held every four years, during every other congressional election.

Most states and localities combine their elections with the federal elections in November, although some do hold separate elections. Their ballots often include proposals and special issues pertaining to their localities. For example, a referendum for funding some public project like a school or swimming pool might show up on the ballot.

Primary elections are those elections in which members of a party select candidates for the general elections, and they are usually held in the spring of the general election year. Most of the states—all but about ten—use a closed primary system, in which only preregistered party members can vote. Independents can vote in most of these elections if they preregister with one party. In a few cases, voters can choose a party and register for that ballot on the day of the vote.

The rest of the states use open primaries, in which voters need not identify their party preference. Registered voters walk into their polling places, choose a party, and vote, although they usually have to vote completely within one party. The primaries in a few states are even more open. Voters can choose candidates for each office from any party represented, in what is called a **blanket primary.**

To get on the ballot in a primary election, a party must have passed a certain threshold in the number of votes it got in the previous presidential or gubernatorial election. In most states, if a party got 5 percent of the votes cast, it qualifies. Candidates can also qualify for primaries by paying a fee or by collecting a certain number of signatures on a petition.

Some states, mostly in the south, have **runoff elections** following primaries, if no candidate receives a majority in the primary. The primary's two top runners face off in this election, which has its roots in a time when the Democratic Party dominated in the south. The runoff effectively replaced the general election, because the opposing parties were irrelevant.

In a few states, party **caucuses** take the place of primaries. Party members gather in small localized groups to decide who to nominate. At the state party conventions, candidates who get a certain percentage of the delegates' votes receive the party's endorsement.

Of course, presidential nominations in the major parties are decided at the national conventions. Delegates who do the nominating are usually selected in party primaries or in caucus/convention systems within the state party organizations. The presidential primary season has now stretched to nearly four months—a grueling period in which candidates ramble from state to state, their campaigns either gaining momentum or dying in the process.

A final catchall category is that of **special elections.** One type of special election is held when officeholders leave office and their positions must be filled. Usually the law requires a fairly expeditious process for these elections, and the vacancies are filled within one to three months. Special elections are held also to deal with pressing issues. For example, voters might have a chance to vote in a special election to say yes or no to an increase in school funding.

Proportional Representation

Two important processes affecting elections, as well as legislative outcomes, are those of **apportionment** and **redistricting.** Apportionment is the method by which House seats are awarded to states, based on their populations, every ten years when the census is completed. The law requires that the number of representatives in the House is to stay at 435, but as some states lose population and others gain it, seats might shift from one state to another. When this happens, congressional districts become smaller or larger, depending on whether a state gains or loses congressional seats. The district boundaries have to be redrawn, so that each representative's district contains roughly the same number of people, and this is referred to as redistricting.

These processes concern only the House of Representative at the federal level and the similar house that exists in almost all states. The Senate, of course, holds equal representation for each state, regardless of population. Each state elects two senators. This was specified in the Constitution, so as to keep populous states from overwhelming the smaller states in the legislative process. In those state legislatures that have a counterpart for the U.S. Senate, the situation is similar, with that house having fewer members, each representing a larger area.

Redistricting has been controversial throughout our history. Governors and legislatures are generally responsible for redrawing the district lines, on both the state and federal level. Parties in control of that process have been known to draw the lines so as to include or exclude certain parts of the population from certain districts. They do this to try to control the makeup of the districts—to try to ensure that they include more voters favoring their party than any other. They thus give themselves a better chance in future elections.

Districts drawn to favor one party over the other do not usually resemble simple boxes on the map. They often have strange looking configurations. In 1812, the party of Massachusetts Governor Eldridge Gerry drew up a district plan that had such a shape. One of the party's opponents said it resembled a salamander, and another critic gave it the label of *gerrymander.* To this day the practice of drawing district lines to favor one party over another is called **gerrymandering.**

In 1982, Congress passed amendments to the 1965 Voting Rights Act that outlawed redistricting based on race. This was done to prevent redistricting plans that would effectively eliminate racial minorities from the political process. Then in 1986, the Supreme Court ruled that gerrymandering violates the Constitution, although it did not specifically delineate what was gerrymandering and what was not. The practice has continued, and in some instances, district lines have been drawn to concentrate minorities to give them majority status within their districts. In a series of cases in the 1990s, the Supreme Court again struck down this process. Now, a district can legally end up having one minority group as its majority. But, according to the Court, race cannot be the primary and predominant factor in drawing the lines. The Court is also trying to influence the process such that districts will be drawn more compactly and logically.

These court cases affect state as well as federal legislative districts. Scores of state and federal districts are consequently subject to being redrawn. Also, parties that feel they have been gerrymandered can sue in court to have their districts redrawn. Issues surrounding redistricting are among the most contentious and challenging for the state legislators who have to settle them. And they remain fundamental to the processes and outcomes of elections and legislation.

In chapter 3, we take a closer look at how elections work. We examine the role of parties, how campaigns work, campaign funding rules, and how political action committees fit in. In chapter 5, we see how this information can be applied to help your credit union and all credit unions. We look at the realities of campaign contributions and how to make the most of them. And, we consider how to build relationships with political candidates as a way to make a foundation for our work with legislators. But at this point, we turn to the questions of how the game of politics affects credit unions and how our involvement in the game can make a difference.

CHAPTER TWO

CREDIT UNIONS AND POLITICS

ORIGINS OF CREDIT UNIONS THROUGH POLITICS

The rich and wonderful history of the credit union movement, both here and around the world, is an inspiring story and one that has been well told elsewhere. The cast of characters should be familiar to anyone who has become involved in perpetuating the credit union philosophy. For purposes of this handbook, however, a brief exploration of that history from a political perspective should deepen your appreciation for the role that politics has taken in the genesis and growth of credit unions. After all, there are some people in credit unions today who don't think we should be involved in the political game. Even a cursory review of our movement's history will show that credit unions have always had to participate in the political arena, beginning with their very creation.

Credit unions began in Europe about the same time that a set of **cooperative principles** were being developed among a group of weavers in Rochdale, England. When the great credit union pioneers Friedrich Raiffeisen and Hermann Schulze-Delitzsch started spreading the idea of credit cooperatives in Germany in the 1800s, they were developing models similar to other early co-ops. Later, these principles and models would be applied to all types of enterprises, such as cooperative farm supply and marketing, rural electric utilities, and others. Nowadays, the cooperative approach to housing, grocery sales, and worker-owned enterprises still serves the same purpose—helping "people of average means" compete with big business. This area of the economy is known as the **cooperative sector,** and contact with other co-ops has helped form important political alliances for credit unions.

Credit unions were first created without the benefit of **enabling legislation.** The early credit union pioneers did not look to the government for the framework or structure of their new enterprises. Instead, the idea of credit unions as providers of financial services on a cooperative basis to people of small means was so powerful that it moved throughout civilization of its own accord. Of course, this was a much simpler time when the "rule of law" did not dominate so many facets of our lives as it does now.

Nevertheless, when Alphonse Dejardins brought the idea to North America and started the first credit unions in Canada, there was no law or regulation allowing that practice. He just saw a need for financial services and had a blueprint for how to provide them to the people that needed them.

As credit unionism spread to America, however, the need for a consistent legal framework was apparent. You have no doubt heard the legend of Edward Filene's role in the birth and development of the credit union movement in the United States, including the fact that he spent more than a million dollars of his own money to foster its growth. Filene was a well-known Boston merchant who was captivated by the idea of credit unions and the good they could perform on behalf of the working class of his time. By about 1910, over a dozen credit unions were organized and operating in Massachusetts. However, early organization efforts were slowed because of several factors.

First, there was no public role in the structure or formation of credit unions. At this time in history, many organizations grew out of the recognition that consumers of the day needed access to financial services. Large employers or communities formed their own savings and lending plans without a consistent framework or set of operating principles. Credit unions were just one form of organization that some of these groups chose to use.

Second, and perhaps most important for purposes of this discussion, the public was naturally skeptical of this newfound financial structure. Innovations in financial services for consumers were usually someone's slick idea of a new way to separate a fool from their money. Without a uniform set of operating standards and qualified managers to apply them, credit union organization was slow.

One of Filene's first steps to jump-start the growth of the credit union movement was to retain Roy Bergengren, a Massachusetts attorney, to head the Massachusetts Credit Union Association (MCUA). Started in 1916, the MCUA's purpose was to aid existing credit unions and to assist in the formation of new ones. The economic hardships of World War I passed into the growing economic prosperity of the United States in the early 1920s. The clamor for consumer credit ignored by the existing banks and savings institutions resounded in the rapidly increasing interest in the idea of credit unions.

To help channel this new interest and spur credit union growth and development, Filene hired Bergengren in 1920 to run the MCUA and develop the structure of credit unions and their support systems throughout the United States. Filene and Bergengren moved quickly beyond the MCUA to formation of the Credit Union National Extension Bureau (CUNEB) in July 1921 to promote credit unions on a national scale. The two pioneers set four ambitious yet simple goals:

1. *Establish enabling legislation.* Filene and Bergengren knew that credit unions would be easier to organize if laws were in place setting out their structure and purpose.
2. *Organize credit unions.* Convince potential member groups like employers and communities that credit unions were the best framework to provide consumer financial services.
3. *Form state leagues.* Organization and chartering activities needed a local support network that could foster cooperation and education among the credit unions, bringing the benefits of cooperative principles to bear across the board.
4. *Form a national organization.* This national league would take cooperation among state leagues to the next level and ensure that credit unions would indeed become a nationwide movement.

For the next thirteen years, Bergengren set to work, with Filene's financial backing, to bring the goals to completion. Little by little, state by state, laws were enacted, credit unions were organized, and leagues were formed. However, even at this early stage, credit unions were not free of political controversy and dissension. One manifestation of this reality was early banker opposition, which arose fullforce in Iowa.

> *Little by little, state by state, laws were enacted, credit unions were organized, and leagues were formed.*

In the late 1920s, a banker quashed an attempt by a priest, Father Roney, to form a credit union for his small Iowa parish. Father Roney and Bergengren trudged through snowdrifts to invite families to an organizing meeting for the credit union. Reportedly, the banker literally followed in their footprints through the snow, warning people not to attend and reminding them of the loans they had with the bank. When Bergengren later asked the banker why he so vehemently opposed credit unions, the banker replied, "What you are doing is banking, and banking is for bankers." Even back then, bankers thought they were entitled to define credit unions and dictate where, when, and to whom they should be able to provide their services. Their battle has moved from Iowa snowdrifts to the white marble halls of Congress, but the message has remained remarkably unchanged.

Despite these and other forms of opposition, early development efforts by Bergengren, funded and directed by Filene, ultimately bore fruit. The culmination of the first organizational stages of credit unions was adoption of the **Federal Credit Union Act.** The bill was first introduced in 1933 and, for just over a year, the document was debated, revised, and debated some more. Passage was accomplished by a grassroots effort from credit union people all over the country urging senators and representatives to support the bill. It passed and was signed into law by Franklin Roosevelt in June of 1934, giving rise to the **dual chartering system,** the option of operating a credit union according to state or federal laws, and bringing to a close the initial period of credit union formation in the United States.

Passage of the Federal Credit Union Act also marked the entrance of credit unions into the national political arena. Pushing for the creation of a federal credit union law meant that credit unions assumed the responsibility to preserve and enhance their enabling legislation as future changes and challenges dictated. Combined with the many states that had already passed their own acts to allow for the creation and organization of credit unions, our early pioneers recognized that credit unions had thrust themselves into the political arena on both the state and national levels.

ROLE OF CREDIT UNIONS AS COOPERATIVES IN POLITICS

As mentioned earlier, credit unions are not unique in using the cooperative form as an organizational structure. Most true cooperatives grew out of the **Rochdale Principles,** a set of guidelines established by the early pioneers who developed the idea of the cooperative form of business. These voluntary principles include open membership, democratic control, service at cost, education, and cooperation among cooperatives. They have been discussed, debated, and reevaluated over the years, but the fundamental principles are still followed by credit unions and other cooperative businesses to this day.

Among these principles is one that calls for **neutrality** in religion and politics. The purpose for this principle is based on the belief that a co-op will be more successful if it can avoid extraneous issues that can seriously divide people who otherwise share a common interest. People don't always agree on religion or politics, but those involved in a cooperative venture like a credit union should focus on the issues that have brought them together and direct their energies at promoting and supporting the good of that organization.

Discussing adherence to this basic principle of political neutrality in a handbook about credit union political action might seem like a contradiction. In fact, credit unions can be neutral on most issues and yet involved in politics at the same time. The point is that credit unions need to focus their involvement narrowly on issues that affect them specifically and relate to their unique structure and purpose. Historically, those national cooperative movements that have become involved in **partisan politics**—supporting one party's positions on issues that did not directly impact them as cooperatives—have suffered when the partisan political winds have changed.

> *Credit unions need to focus their involvement narrowly on issues that affect them specifically.*

The other potentially divisive element that participation in partisan politics creates is among your members. If a political issue is particularly prominent, it's tempting for your credit union to jump on the bandwagon and support that prominent cause in an effort to raise your profile in the community. But unless there's near unanimity among your members and potential members on that issue, the defections from disenchanted members may well outbalance any gain you make from a populist appeal.

More important, once your credit union has crossed that line and taken a position on an issue that's outside of its limited scope, you open the door to challenges and invitations on future issues that may be just as divisive but not as uniformly held by your members. That's why credit unions historically have narrowly focused their political efforts on issues directly and uniquely affecting them and their business. Individual, personal political positions need to be respected and encouraged, but when acting in an official capacity or on behalf of the credit union, keep the focus on those particular issues.

The cooperative principle of nonpartisanship carries both positive and negative consequences. On the positive side, it does galvanize and focus our political efforts. Credit unions know where to direct their efforts and what battles to fight if they stick to this clear definition of our political message. With a limited goal to accomplish in the political game, our efforts are more effective and our purpose and direction are clearer. It's easier to accomplish one or two direct political tasks than to get bogged down in struggles over issues that affect broader social groups.

The negative consequences can be rather dramatic, however. In chapter 3, we'll discuss the partisan nature of American politics and the important role political parties play in the selection, promotion, and election of candidates. Party politics drive the formation of legislative agendas and allocation of attention by legislative leaders, all of whom are selected according to party affiliation or position. If credit unions fail to get involved directly in supporting the party in power, that party will be more reluctant to push credit union concerns near the top of its political agenda. After all, it's true in so many facets of life—you scratch my back, I'll scratch yours. If credit unions refuse to assist party efforts, why should the party help credit unions?

The answer to this dilemma is difficult. We're one of the few politically active groups that are neutral with regard to parties and ideologies. However, the history of credit union political action has demonstrated that we've been able to succeed throughout times when either Republicans or Democrats governed the process. That's why broad-based political involvement is again so crucial for credit unions, because we have twice as much work to do in educating candidates and cultivating relationships since we have to cover both sides of the aisle.

HISTORY AND EVOLUTION OF CREDIT UNION POLITICAL ACTION

The mission and purpose behind credit union political action has changed dramatically through the years, as credit unions themselves have adopted different roles in the financial services marketplace. Early efforts were directed at establishing the organizational structure and framework for credit unions. Credit union acts were passed in most states, the only exceptions being Delaware, South Dakota, and Wyoming.

Once the dual chartering option was established for practically all credit unions, leagues and credit unions turned to building their niche in the marketplace. Cooperative education and resources were developed that allowed the message of credit unions to spread. The success of that effort was demonstrated with the explosive growth in the number of credit unions all over the country.

As credit unions expanded in number, their prominence in political circles started to rise. Consumer financial services assumed a new focus after World War II, when economic prosperity spread to the burgeoning middle class. The baby boom brought with it demands for credit to purchase automobiles, home appliances, and other relatively small-dollar items. This created a consumer market in which credit unions flourished. Our continued growth through this period led to increased political prominence and a larger stake in the legislative scene. Along the way, numerous challenges were issued and beat back by the combined political activism of credit unions.

The first significant threat was a challenge to the credit union tax exemption mounted by the bankers in the late 1940s and early 1950s. At that time, the financial services marketplace was populated by a variety of banking organizations, each of which operated within a defined niche and pretty much stayed out of each others' way. Banks provided commercial credit and services, thrifts provided home loans, and credit unions were the consumer credit provider of choice. Banks and thrifts were heavily regulated institutions with limited powers and opportunities for growth.

The growing consumer market created an opportunity that banks and thrifts decided they wanted to exploit. Mutual banks and thrifts at this time traded off their income tax exemption for the expanded powers they needed to take advantage of the growing economic boom. Credit unions stuck to their consumer niche and did not approach Congress for these increased powers. Despite strong efforts by the banks and thrifts to drag credit unions into this financial institution restructuring in powers and tax treatment, credit unions were left unchanged.

The 1960s saw a dramatic rise in credit union prominence that matched the increased consumer market. Credit unions successfully lobbied Congress for establishment of an independent federal regulator and share insurance fund. Our unique structure and purpose required a regulator that understood and supported these directions, and credit unions finally reached critical mass to justify this independent role.

Consumers continued to demand a greater variety of financial services, and credit unions grew to the point that we could meet that demand. In the 1970s, the battle was joined over share drafts, the credit union equivalent of checking accounts. Credit unions needed enabling legislation to guarantee the right to provide this type of service, and they initiated a nationwide lobbying campaign called "Save Our Share Drafts." Congress had to face down strong opposition from the bankers in passing that law.

But Congress would soon need to address larger problems in the financial services arena. Rampant inflation in the late 1970s led to deregulation of financial institutions in the early 1980s so they could compete with other financial services providers that weren't as hidebound by complex regulations and limitations. While this deregulation provided opportunities for some financial institutions, it also triggered the death of others that failed to adopt the strategies necessary for survival. Credit unions devised cooperative solutions in the area of deregulation and recapitalization of our deposit insurance fund. These changes allowed credit unions to adapt and survive the changing financial services marketplace.

> *Credit unions devised cooperative solutions. Changes allowed credit unions to adapt and survive the changing financial services marketplace.*

The savings and loan crisis that swept the marketplace later that decade led to tremendous concern by Congress that credit unions and banks would be the next to go. Their proposal to throw us all together and hope enough would survive led to calls for a single regulator and insurance fund. "Operation Grassroots" was a broad-based credit union response to this political challenge. This campaign culminated in a rally on the Capitol Mall in February 1991 that was coordinated with the largest signature petition drive Congress had ever seen in support of preserving the credit union's unique structure and regulation.

Successful efforts such as "Save Our Share Drafts" and "Operation Grassroots" demonstrated the political power that credit unions could muster when challenged. They gave rise to an expanded political consciousness and an awareness of our collective impact on political issues.

The "Campaign for Consumer Choice" was an echo of those earlier struggles. Once again, in 1997–98, we asked Congress to recognize and support the credit union's mission of providing cooperative financial services to consumers who choose that option.

As this brief history demonstrates, credit unions have relied on Congress and state legislatures for years—first in defining our organization, and then providing the framework within which we can accomplish our mission for our members. We've only been successful in the past because some crisis has galvanized our efforts. Now, we seem to live in a constant state of political crisis. Coordinated, consistent efforts are necessary to survive into the future.

CREDIT UNIONS' POLITICAL/LEGISLATIVE FRAMEWORK

To truly appreciate the role credit unions have in the political arena, you need to recognize all the areas of your credit union that are at play. Credit unions are created by law, defined by law, governed by law, operated by law, restricted by law, and, when necessary, closed and liquidated by law. And, as you no doubt know by now, those laws are passed, amended, or repealed by legislatures, which are run according to the rules of the game of politics.

The fact that your credit union exists is owed to an enabling statute passed either by Congress, if your credit union is federally chartered, or your state legislature, if it's state-chartered. The credit union act defines your credit union's purpose. The law determines the credit union's structure—including the board, committees, and management officers, for example—and characteristics—such as a volunteer board and not-for-profit status. Powers are also spelled out for the credit union and its board or management, as are legal requirements for its continued operation. Typically, some form of regulatory structure is established.

The government agency by which the credit union is supervised is also a creature of the legislature, which has created the bureaucratic structure, defined the agency's purpose, provided it with funding, and established its operating powers and procedures. Chief among these powers is usually the authority to write regulations that pertain to its regulated entities. These regulations can only be enforced in the areas to which the legislature has delegated the agency authority to regulate. Regulations can also be superceded or amended by subsequent legislative action.

The legislature can also enact laws that affect credit union operations, even in areas not directly affecting credit unions. Many legislatures have passed **consumer protection laws,** with enabling rules written by the appropriate agency. Credit unions must follow these laws if they are to be in the business of providing consumer financial services. The laws don't apply uniquely or specifically to credit unions, but by choosing to provide those services, we also must recognize that those laws and rules will govern our actions.

Similarly, credit unions are also governed by state and federal laws that apply to businesses in general—like minimum wage, workplace safety, and equal employment opportunity. Again, these laws don't pertain to credit unions alone but to anyone who chooses to do business in that state or country. As credit unions expand to become ever-larger members of the business community, more and more of these laws will control or direct how you, as an employer, run your credit union.

In becoming active players in the political game, therefore, we must identify all laws that affect, directly or indirectly, our ability to fulfill our purpose—providing cooperative financial services to members. The list of laws is broad and ever-increasing as government regulates all businesses to a greater degree over time. But these laws set the boundaries in our game; they're the foundation for the playing field on which we'll operate. Remember our earlier explanation of the importance of focusing on only those political issues pertinent to your credit union. These laws will lead you to know what those issues are.

Role of Credit Union Leagues/CUNA

No discussion of the role of credit unions in politics would be complete without talking about two important players in the political game—your **league** and the **Credit Union National Association (CUNA)**. These two organizations have the responsibility of coordinating and directing all credit union political action.

You might ask why this authority should be vested in these organizations. In other words, who elected these guys? Well, the simple answer is, you did. Credit unions recognized early on that they needed to unify their power in the political arena if they were to be successful. Trade associations like your league and CUNA provide methods by which any group of businesses in a particular industry band together. Typically, there are trade associations for doctors, dentists, restaurants, home builders, small businesses, and, yes, even the bankers. These associations often evolve different functions depending on the industry they represent and their members' demands and expectations. Our credit union trade associations, like their other trade association brethren, exist to fulfill a political role by galvanizing and directing their members' governmental affairs activities.

Leagues are very similar in structure and operation to your credit union. They are operated on a nonprofit basis and are exempt from federal income tax. Leagues are governed by a volunteer board that is elected by its membership to establish policies and direction, just as your credit union's board does. Membership in these organizations is made up of credit unions within the league's area of operation. Your state league represents member credit unions in your state; CUNA represents the state leagues and credit unions from a national perspective. Both are supported financially by dues, which members pay to support the organizations' efforts on their behalf.

The basic mission of leagues and CUNA, as trade associations, is to represent the credit union industry to the public in general and the government in particular. The structure and purpose of a trade association are limited by federal tax law and by applicable state laws that govern its organization and powers, just as they do your credit union. Leagues are restricted to basically providing governmental affairs, education, and public relations services to their members.

Depending on the degree of support and cooperation they receive from their members, leagues often branch beyond these basic missions to facilitate the cooperative efforts of credit unions to provide financial services. Leagues, and sometimes their credit unions, invest in outside subsidiaries that provide these services to credit unions outside the nonprofit structure of the league as a trade association. But these service corporations are outside of the trade association structure, governed by different tax laws, and run as for-profit businesses.

CUNA is the trade association representing credit unions before Congress and the national media. Other countries with active credit union movements also have national counterparts like CUNA that provide representation to all the credit unions in those countries. Your state league is a member of CUNA, and represents you directly to your state government and to your federal representatives and senators. Education and public relations efforts vary from state to state depending on your league's resources and expertise, but CUNA also provides this role on a national level on behalf of all credit unions in the United States.

CUNA's governmental affairs structure starts with its board, which sets policies in this area as in every other area within the organization. Because of the importance of the governmental affairs function within CUNA, its board has appointed a **Governmental Affairs Committee** that specializes in this area. The committee is made up of people with a particular expertise or interest in governmental affairs. They meet periodically and make policy recommendations to the CUNA board. Input and direction on CUNA's governmental affairs efforts often start with, or are run through, the Governmental Affairs Committee as the experts in the area. Your state league probably has a similar structure for decisions in its governmental affairs activities.

Aside from CUNA and your state league, several other associations and ancillary groups have sprung up to represent more narrow interests of credit unions. The National Association of Federal Credit Unions (NAFCU) focuses on the issues that affect federal credit unions only. Its efforts center on Congress. This association does not have a network of state leagues like CUNA, so it takes a less active role in state governmental affairs, even though several issues that affect federal credit unions, such as the consumer protection or business issues we addressed earlier, are also present at a state level.

Another organization of prominence similar to NAFCU is the National Association of State Credit Union Supervisors (NASCUS). NASCUS started as the trade association for state credit union regulators, but has developed a state credit union council that represents the interests of state-chartered credit unions before Congress and federal agencies.

Both NAFCU and NASCUS take a more narrow view of credit union interests than do CUNA or your state league, which represent all credit unions regardless of charter. In the political arena, these organizations can create some confusion if they send conflicting messages to legislators, which can happen if the particular issue has facets that create conflict among the groups' members. It's incumbent on all of these organizations—and those others that represent even narrower interests within the credit union community—to clearly define what group they represent and what their particular interest in the issue might be. Even with careful coordination, multiple voices can fracture our unified voice in Congress and the legislature. So the challenge, which will shape the future role of credit unions in politics, is to bring these diverse voices together in concert and to strongly articulate the credit union position. Only through united political action will we continue to protect our role as financial cooperatives.

CHAPTER THREE

ELECTIONS

Those who play the game of politics professionally get their jobs by winning elections, or by being appointed to public office by the winners of elections. For amateurs who wish to have some influence in the political game, the key is to build relationships with the professional players. In other words, to influence the outcome of the political process, we need to influence our legislative representatives. It serves well in pursuing that goal to have helped a representative to win an election. Long before they actually move into their offices, the relationship-building and influencing process can begin.

This chapter takes a closer look at the election process and how it fits into the big picture. We examine this particular part of the game of politics, starting with the players and the teams.

POLITICAL PARTIES AND CANDIDATES

Like professional sports teams, the major political parties have developed huge and complex organizations. They have the extremely challenging tasks of recruiting and nominating candidates, raising money, informing and motivating voters, and campaigning for the election of their nominees. All of that work takes more and more money, time, and human effort every year. At one time, parties did their work mostly during the periodic election season, and that is still the case at the county level. But with politics becoming more of a high-stakes, competitive venture every year, those who run the parties at the national and state levels are more likely to be working full time.

> *The major political parties have developed huge and complex organizations.*

At the top of each major party organization is a national committee, which directs the party's business and plans and runs the national convention. Attending the convention are the party's most active members—its delegates—who have the tasks of nominating the presidential candidates, establishing the rules, and writing the party platforms. Next down in the party's hierarchy are the state committees, which perform the same functions at the state level. They hold state party conventions, again made up of delegates chosen by the party rank and file. The third level down is that of the county committees. In some parts of the country there are legislative district committees, wards, and precincts, each of which has its officers.

Parties are not as powerful as they once were. In much of the nineteenth and part of the twentieth centuries, party politics were dominated by a form of organization known as the **machine.** It depended on the party controlling public resources and channeling them to their supporters and away from their opponents. In this **spoils system,** public jobs were often given to loyal party workers. In some cities and counties, construction contracts went to companies that were loyal and generous to the party in power. Reforms such as the direct primary, which took the nomination power away from party committees and gave it to party members, seriously weakened the machines. The merit system for civil service hiring and promotion became widely adopted in the 1910s and 1920s and destroyed the spoils system in most states.

As parties have lost some of the power they once had, the focus of many election campaigns has shifted away from the parties and toward the candidates. Candidates now often set up their own offices and organizations and raise their own funds for campaigning. While they may not disengage from their parties, they don't rely on them for all resources as they did in the past. They may work the issues independently and in different ways than others in their parties. Modern mass media tools—radio, television, direct marketing, and the Internet—make this independence easier to achieve. Nevertheless, they still need money and lots of it, and for that, many candidates still rely heavily on the parties. With the advent of massive use of **soft money**—money originally given to parties for party building and political education purposes—the party connection has regained its importance for many candidates.

While the power of the parties has ebbed and flowed, they are still firmly entrenched in the political process. On the national and state levels, serious candidates almost always have a major party affiliation. Of course, there are the extraordinary individuals who run and win as independents. But most people need the resources—people power, information, and money—that political parties can muster. Those who seek political office, then, usually try to gain the support of the party they prefer, or the party they feel will give them what they need in resources.

As much as the candidates need the party affiliations, the parties also need good candidates to gain power or to stay in power. Some strategically oriented party leaders seek out those who are thought to be good potential candidates, offering the support and resources of the party. For citizens or interest groups, within or outside of a party, this can be the ultimate beginning of a relationship in which they might have the most influence over the political process. What better way to have a hand in the game than to recruit and train one of the players and to work to get that player into the game?

Hence, parties obtain candidates by recruiting them and, more often, by taking on candidates who sign up with them to run for office. Once it has a list of candidates for any given office, the party's next job is to nominate one of them to take part in the election for that office. Parties do this by means of primary elections, caucuses, and conventions.

As we saw in chapter 1, the direct primary election is the most common method of nomination. All voters in a designated area—whether it is a county, a legislative district, or the entire nation—directly choose the nominee for the party. Candidates wishing to appear on the ballot must file papers with whatever state agency regulates the primaries. As a part of filing, they must pay a fee and/or file a petition signed by a certain required number of people from their districts who support their candidacy.

In some states, the requirements regarding deadlines and supporting documents are more stringent and complex than in others. For example, in 1996, New York's requirements for getting on the Republican presidential primary ballot became notorious. Each candidate had to have the support of three party delegates to the national convention, along with three alternate delegates, from each of thirty-one congressional districts. Also from each of those districts, each candidate had to collect 1,250 signatures of registered party members, and all signers had to sign in exactly the same fashion as they had signed upon registering to vote. These signatures had to be collected between Thanksgiving Day of 1995 and January 4, 1996. Finally, each of the thirty-one petitions had to be submitted to a separate elections board. Most states' requirements are not this stringent.

A less common method of nomination is the party caucus, also discussed in chapter 1. Party members actually assemble in one large group or in several small groups to choose a candidate. In some cases, the smaller caucus groups choose delegates who in turn go to a state convention to elect a nominee.

Of course, throughout this process, each party has to raise a great deal of money. This aspect of the game, more than any other, has soured many eligible voters toward the whole system. During any campaign season, we hear almost every day about another $1000-a-plate fund-raising dinner being held somewhere in the country, with politicians dining and rubbing shoulders with wealthy party patrons. Then we might look in the mailbox and find yet another envelope from a party or a candidate with urgent pleading for $25, $35, $100, or whatever we can afford to help ensure victory in the next election.

For any major party, it seems to many that the political messages have been replaced, or at least overwhelmed, by the pitch for donations. But like it or not, raising money has become an integral part of the political game, and serious players need to acknowledge that fact and learn how to work with it. We explore the role of money in politics, and how organizations use it to their advantage, as we proceed in this handbook.

With its slate of nominees for the next election, the ultimate job for any political party is to inform, motivate, and mobilize the voters. The end of that process—mobilizing voters—takes practical forms. It involves getting voters registered and getting them out to vote. In the weeks before the election, party activists talk on the phone and walk door-to-door, encouraging people to register and giving them information on how to do it. On election day, it can mean actually transporting people who need a ride to the polling places.

Long before election day, however, the more complex part of the process—informing and motivating voters—begins. It is long and grueling, and it can become tiresome to political participants as well as to voters. It is that part of the political game referred to as the campaign.

THE CAMPAIGN

Candidates and parties need to inform voters about their views and values regarding the issues of the day. They need to motivate voters, not only to vote for them but also to become active politically and to support them by promoting their candidacy to others. Informing voters and motivating them are the primary purposes of a campaign.

Campaigners need to get their messages across to as many voters as possible in a limited amount of time. In the earliest days of our country's history, that meant getting the candidate before groups of people, traveling on foot, in a horse-drawn carriage, and, in the most extravagant campaigns, by train. It meant printing the message on an old-fashioned printing press for circulation among hundreds or maybe thousands of voters. Nowadays it means a lot more.

The candidates still have to get themselves before people, but now they travel in much wider circles, and often by jet plane. The message is still going out on printed flyers, but it is also going via newspapers, magazines, mass mailings, the telephone, the radio, and, most importantly, via television. The latest delivery channel is the Internet. And the message is going out to tens of millions of people.

Use of Mass Media

Modern-day campaign tactics have evolved dramatically as the game of politics has grown more complex. Some would say they have grown steadily more unsavory over the years and that the whole process is out of control. The small crowd that once gathered at the train stop has grown to an audience of millions. The megaphone has been replaced by electronic media. The documentary has been replaced by the sound bite. And campaign budgets have swelled to ridiculous proportions.

Early in the era of mass communication, politicians employed filmmakers to record newsreels in dramatic and emotionally moving styles. Since then, they have hired personal image trainers to mold themselves to fit what public opinion seems to demand and to make them as charismatic and appealing as they can be. They have brought in consultants who study competing strategies and adopt them—or co-opt them—for their own use. Wizards of database technology are hired to tap the huge small-donor segment through sophisticated market research and target marketing methods. And, reminiscent of the early moving picture days, professional videographers now cast television ads to have maximum emotional impact on their viewers, usually in thirty-second segments.

Almost all modern methods of campaigning depend on some sort of mass media technology. Reporters follow the candidates and report on their campaigns in newspapers and magazines, and on radio and television. Likewise, political debates are covered live on local and national television and radio. **Incumbents**—those already holding office and seeking reelection—have the advantage here. By simply doing their jobs, and doing them with a careful eye to how the media will cover their performances, they can get a lot more exposure than their challengers can. But incumbents and challengers do not simply wait for journalists to spread their messages via straight news coverage. As mass communication becomes faster and ever-more pervasive, serious players have to become more active.

Today's candidates need to be clever about mass media in order to compete. They need to know how to use the media. Savvy campaigners now stage events to attract news coverage in what has come to be known as the **photo opportunity.** Political ad making for national and local media has become an industry. More and more serious candidates and parties have web pages for those potential voters who frequent the Internet. And candidates are now making use of radio and television talk shows as a way to get their messages out without having to face probing journalists.

Use of Polling and Public Opinion

Communication is a two-way street, and candidates cannot just broadcast their messages and expect to win. They also have to know how the people are receiving their messages. This can be difficult because public opinion is not easy to define at any one time, nor is it easy to measure. Once measured, it can change overnight depending on events. Nevertheless, politicians try very hard to gauge public opinion on critical issues as they campaign for nomination and for public office. They employ professional pollsters, and they often fire them when their campaigns begin to falter. They read letters to the editor, and they pay attention to what influential **public opinion leaders**—editorial writers, political pundits, entertainers, and others—are saying about them and about issues of the day. Some politicians adjust their messages to suit what the public seems to want as part of their campaign strategies.

The use of public opinion has become an interesting part of the political game, because strategists from all sides are making use of it. Most of us have seen ads and received mail from groups supporting particular causes. We have very likely all been approached to sign petitions for one cause or another. And, of course, it is hard to avoid unsolicited phone calls from political groups, especially around election time.

Interest groups try to mold public opinion, sometimes very aggressively, and thereby influence politicians indirectly by getting the rest of us to influence them. Sometimes, if these groups get too aggressive, their efforts backfire and do more harm than good for their causes. Hence, candidates and those who support them need to be aware of what interest groups are saying about them, and they need to know how to react.

Again, incumbents have a decided advantage in this whole process, for several reasons:

- They usually have many times more exposure to the public than their challengers do. Just by doing their jobs, they make the newspapers and talk shows.
- Most of them have more experience in government than their challengers do. They have spent at least two years learning the ins and outs and what they can and cannot promise; they simply know how to play the game better than most opponents do.
- They have easier access to more information than many of their challengers do. Their staffs work full time to help them with their government jobs, and they can use the fruits of that labor in their campaigns, while challengers and their supporters have to get that information for themselves.
- Incumbents have the ability to do good things for their constituents by channeling public funds into projects that benefit their districts.
- Not the least of the incumbents' advantages is the **franking privilege**—the ability to send official mail at taxpayer expense. While they cannot use this money expressly for campaigning, their newsletters and responses to constituent inquiries are never written in such a way as to hurt their election chances.
- Probably the most important advantage that incumbents hold is the built-in support they get in raising campaign funds. By holding office, they have the guaranteed attention of people and organizations that want to influence the political process, and that have money to contribute. Again, just by showing up for work, they get the opportunity to build relationships with people who can help them to get their jobs done and to get reelected. Challengers have to work harder to find those relationships.

Every stage of every campaign costs money—more and more every year. The dramatic growth in the scope of campaigns has brought us to the point where they cost more in terms of money, time, and people power than they ever have before. At the national level, and increasingly at the state level, the costs of campaigning have become too high for most citizens to consider. The center of the game of politics has become limited to those who can marshal the resources needed to finance and carry out an aggressive campaign. Just how they gather those resources is subject to certain rules.

> *Every stage of every campaign costs money—more and more every year.*

Rules of the Game

The laws governing campaign finance on the federal level began to take shape in 1971 with the passage of the **Federal Election Campaign Act (FECA).** Before that time, candidates were free to take donations of any size and there were no limits on how much money they could raise and spend. The 1971 law instituted such limits. Under FECA, no individual can contribute more than $1,000 to any one congressional candidate in any one election. One individual can give up to $20,000 per year to a national party committee and no more than $5,000 per year to any other political committee. The maximum that one person can give in any one year to election campaigns is $25,000.

FECA put severe limits on individual donors who would give enormous amounts of money to campaigns. It also allowed for greater political activity among interest groups by expanding the use of the political action committee (PAC). PACs are described and discussed in more detail later in this and other chapters. The donation limit for individuals to PACs was set at $5,000 per federal election campaign.

Many states passed laws modeled after FECA to control spending in state elections. The level of reform in the states varies, and sometimes it takes a crisis to get real reform. For example, Kentucky once had among the least-stringent campaign finance limits in the country. An FBI investigation found corruption at the highest levels of state government, resulting in the conviction of the speaker of the state house of representatives. As a result of the scandal, the state passed sweeping legislation and now has one of the most stringent campaign finance laws in the country.

As a result of FECA and similar state laws, candidates were forced to shift their attention from a relatively small number of wealthy contributors to a much larger segment of the population. This was the advent of gigantic fund-raising efforts. Political parties and candidates began to make use of computerized mass mailing to solicit contributions from as many people as possible.

FECA obviously did not slow campaign fund-raising and spending. In 1972, the year after the law was passed, presidential candidates Nixon and McGovern each raised more than did any other presidential candidate in history. Concerns over this led to a strengthening of the law with the 1974 amendments to FECA.

The 1974 amendments extended FECA spending limits to presidential campaigns and expanded the system of public financing. During their campaigns for nomination, eligible candidates can get $250 from the government for every $250 they get from a private contributor. Also, parties of a certain size can get federal funding for the election campaigns. The amendments also put a limit on the total amount of money candidates can spend during the nomination and election campaigns.

In 1975, the **Federal Election Commission (FEC)** was established to enforce the rules. It was mandated to encourage voluntary compliance with election laws. One way the FEC does that is by auditing campaign financial data and publishing its findings. It is also in charge of registering and monitoring PACs. The chief criticism of the FEC is that Congress controls it rather tightly. It is a watchdog whose subjects are also its masters.

The rules of campaign funding were dramatically changed again in 1976 by the court case of *Buckley v. Valeo*. The Supreme Court ruled that while contributions to a campaign can be limited, the government cannot regulate **independent expenditures.** This is spending by groups or individuals on behalf of a candidate without the formal permission or approval of the candidate. An independent expenditure might also be used to broadcast information or opinions about an issue, which indirectly supports a candidate without naming the candidate. Thus, groups favoring a candidate but not working directly for the campaign can spend as much as they want.

Also, the Buckley decision made an exception to FECA, which holds that presidential candidates taking public money for their campaigns can spend no more than $50,000 of their own money. The Court held that candidates who do not accept public funding can spend as much of their own money as they desire. Candidates who have taken advantage of this include Ross Perot in 1992 and Steve Forbes in 1996. Perot took public money and abided by the limits in his 1996 campaign.

One more significant event that helped to shape the campaign financing rules was the passage of the 1979 amendments to FECA. These amendments allowed parties to collect unlimited sums of soft money—money intended for strengthening party organizations and for mobilizing voters through registration drives and get-out-the-vote drives. Instead, the money has been used by both parties to fund campaigns. The Republican and Democratic parties have each spent well over $150 million in soft money in campaigns since the 1979 amendments.

It seems likely that the rules of the campaign finance game will keep changing.

Soft money, like other inventions of Congress, was intended to improve the system—to increase voter participation by helping the parties to encourage it. Like other inventions, it has been used in ways not intended and has therefore become the focus of those who wish to reform campaign financing in our political system. As we head into the new century, campaign financing and the need for reform are among the most troubling issues for Americans. While Congress has been slow to act on this issue lately, it seems likely that the rules of the campaign finance game will keep changing.

Another set of rules is aimed at controlling gift-giving. In 1995, Congress responded to a growing controversy by adopting rules that make it harder for them to receive favors from individuals and groups. Senators are now prohibited from receiving gifts worth more than $50 from lobbyists. Representatives, under House rules, cannot accept gifts of over $10 from anyone other than family members and friends. In the next chapter, we take a closer look at lobbying and at other rules pertaining to it. Rules of campaign finance are summarized in figure 3.1.

INTRODUCTION TO POLITICAL ACTION COMMITTEES

As a result of the campaign finance reforms, one of the most important developments in the political arena has been the emergence and growth of the **political action committee (PAC)**. The PAC that we know today was another

Figure 3.1 Limits on Political Contributions

- Limit on what one person can contribute to a federal candidate per each election: $1,000.
- Maximum that one can give per year to a national party committee: $20,000.
- Limit on what one can give to any other political committee in a year: $5,000.
- Maximum that one can give per year to all election campaigns: $25,000.
- Donation limit for PACs: $5,000 per federal election campaign.
- Eligible presidential candidates can get $250 from the government for every $250 they get from a private contributor.
- Presidential candidates taking public money for their campaigns can spend no more than $50,000 of their own money.
- Senators are prohibited from receiving gifts worth more than $50 from lobbyists.
- Representatives cannot accept gifts of over $10 from anyone other than family members and friends.

invention, part of the reform legislation of the early 1970s, that was intended to make the political system more accessible to citizens and less susceptible to the influence of wealthy individuals. Prior to reforms, it had been allowed only for labor unions, and with the changes to the law, interest groups of all kinds were allowed to set up PACs to channel contributions from their members to candidates.

Instituting PACs within the federal law had two purposes. It allowed groups of people with common interests to pool their money for contributions and thereby to compete with wealthy contributors. Of course, with the same legislation, limits were placed on all contributors. So another purpose was to add accountability to the campaign finance system by requiring that all contributions come from identifiable sources, and that all sources keep and disclose detailed records of their contributions.

Interest groups quickly made use of the law, and PACs proliferated. They totaled as many as forty-two hundred in the 1980s, according to studies of PACs

(Squire et al. 1997). The number has since fluctuated around four thousand. Corporations, for example, fit the definition of "people with a common interest." Corporate PACs make up roughly 40 percent of the total number, and they give the most in contributions. PACs representing trade, membership, and health associations generally give the next highest amount, followed by labor PACs, and finally a group of PACs referred to as "nonconnected," or legally independent, from established interest groups.

PAC spending has increased over time, but not all PAC money goes to contributions. For example, the total spending doubled in the twelve years before the 1993–94 election season, in which PACs spent $387 million. Almost half of that money went to administrative and fund-raising expenses, however, with the rest available for contributions. Most of that money goes to congressional candidates, with a small percentage reserved for presidential races. Typically, between 1 and 2 percent of PAC expenditures are for independent expenditures—those dollars spent in support of or in opposition to some candidate without any direct connection to any campaign.

Studies also show that most PACs take a pragmatic approach to their decisions about whom to support, and most of them spend a lot of money on both parties. Their decisions tend to be made on a case-by-case basis. They want to support the winners. They also want to build relationships with as many legislators as they can to give their interest groups the best chance of getting the attention of the legislators. They also give much more money to incumbents, on average, than they do to challengers. And they give disproportionate amounts of money to party leaders and committee chairs (Squire et al. 1997).

Certain classes of PACs, like labor PACs, tend to support one party over another, if it is clear that money spent on the other party would be wasted. For any PAC, it is wise not to give money to anyone and everyone. Smart lobbyists working for the PAC will know which legislators are likely to be supportive, which ones are undecided but might be convinced, and which ones are certainly not going to be supportive.

PACs are currently prohibited from giving more than $5,000 to any one federal election campaign. Primary, runoff, general, and special elections are all considered separately. Each PAC must be registered with the FEC, must have at least fifty donors, and must contribute to at least five candidates for federal office. Presidential candidates who accept public financing—the great majority of all candidates—are also limited by the $5,000-per-PAC rule.

Federally registered PACs are also limited by instruments called **permission agreements,** which are designed to control the amount of soliciting within organizations by PACs that work on behalf of the organizations. Companies and organizations can give permission to only one such PAC per year to ask their members for donations. Because employees might tend to feel obligated to donate whenever asked, this control is intended to prevent circumvention of PAC limits by employers.

Predictably, the states vary greatly in their campaign finance laws. Some follow the federal government and require that interest groups use PACs and give detailed disclosures of contributions. Others do not. In the late 1990s, states generally began to control PACs more strictly. PACs are more active in state governments these days, due to the federal government's attempts to return more money and power to the states. States are generally monitoring PAC activities more closely.

Regardless of the popular conception that PACs are in the business of buying legislators, that characterization seems to be an exaggeration. Political scientists who study these issues argue that there is no direct relationship between PAC contributions and votes on particular issues. This is further supported by testimony of contributors and candidates. The reason seems to be the $5,000 limit on contributions. In a time when campaigns cost millions of dollars, one or even several contributions can hardly be enough to outweigh all other factors. The purchase price for a vote would have to be a lot higher than $5,000 or $25,000 for most legislators to risk the stigma of being "for sale."

What the PAC contributions do seem to buy is access to legislators. They form a big part of the relationship-building process. A contribution gets you the proverbial "foot in the door," and most legislators will at least listen to you if they know you have supported them with a contribution. We look at this and what it means to credit unions more specifically in chapter 6. Ironically, if the contributions buy access rather than votes, they are much less of a threat than the average citizen realizes, and the PAC rules might actually be beneficial to the political process. As much as they help campaign funds, they also force interest groups and organizations to be politically attuned and active, and they cause the politicians to be more responsive to the groups.

If PAC contributions make politicians more responsive, then maybe they do benefit the system, at least as far as the interest groups are concerned. If enough interest groups can gain access, perhaps the needs of most people will be balanced in the political process. This is debatable. But although campaign finance reform may change the way PACs are allowed to operate, it probably will never do away with them. After all, they were instituted to improve the system. As with many such reforms, they were not used exactly as intended; some say they have been abused. But their essential purposes—to give political access to groups that did not have it and to add accountability to the system—will have to remain as part of any reforms. Hence PACs are probably here to stay and will continue to be used by players of the political game.

CHAPTER FOUR

THE LEGISLATIVE PROCESS

The legislative process starts officially with a **bill**, or a document that proposes a new law or a change in the law. The idea for the bill can come from anyone, including you, your next door neighbor, or the President of the United States. Usually, the ideas come from interest groups, executive agencies, members of Congress, and the president. The interest groups referred to here have infinite variety. Many laws have come about because organizations of all stripes—corporate, private, and public—are vitally concerned and knowledgeable about the laws affecting their interests and have been motivated to pursue the process. In this chapter we'll discuss the federal process. It's much the same in each state, with only slight variations.

> *Many laws have come about because organizations are vitally concerned and knowledgeable about the laws affecting their interests.*

HOW A BILL BECOMES A LAW

A bill can be introduced at any time during a session in either house of Congress, but only by a member of that house. The Constitution provides one other limit on how bills are introduced: All bills for raising revenue have to start in the House of Representatives, although the Senate can propose amendments. By tradition, spending bills also originate in the House of Representatives. In the House, the bill goes into the "hopper," a wooden box on the floor of the House. In the Senate the bill is simply registered with a clerk. The senator or representative introducing the bill is called the **sponsor,** and any number of his or her colleagues can sign on as **cosponsors.** Together, sponsors and cosponsors become the champions of the bill.

Once filed, the bill gets assigned a code, which includes "H.R." followed by a number, for House bills, or "S." followed by a number for Senate bills. Usually, the number indicates how many bills have been introduced to that point in the legislative session. So, for example, H.R.100 is usually the one hundredth bill introduced into the House of Representatives. After the introduction of the bill, the Government Printing Office prints it and distributes copies.

Bills almost always get assigned to one of the standing committees of the House or Senate. The presiding officers—the Speaker of the House and the President of the Senate—decide which committees will get the bills. Some committees have clearly defined areas of responsibility, and the assignment is obvious. For example, the Credit Union Membership Access Act (H.R. 1151) was assigned to the House Committee on Banking and Financial Services. Committees in turn usually assign bills to subcommittees, where either the bill meets its end or the real work begins.

Most bills in fact do not get past the subcommittee stage. Indeed, in an average two-year session, around thirteen thousand bills are introduced in each house; a relative handful become laws. From this point on, any bill can simply die if no action is taken. If it gets no action by the end of the two-year period in which each Congress meets, it ceases to exist, and it must be reintroduced in the next session. In subcommittee, at least one member must take interest in the bill in order for it to be considered. Even then, if the chair wishes not to pursue the bill, it might not be taken up for discussion. It might instead be set aside, which is referred to as **tabling.** Unless it gets tabled, its first real action is a **hearing,** in which subcommittee members hear the details of the proposed legislation. At this point, persons and groups affected by the proposal can air their concerns or show their support for the bill.

The next phase is called the **markup session.** Some time after the hearings, the subcommittee or committee meets to mark up the bill—to put it in a form in which it can be released to the floor for debate. This can mean very few or many changes, and it can involve changes that are small or large. In markup, the subcommittee members might change the bill or simply send it unchanged to the full committee. The full committee considers the actions of its subcommittee and may subject the bill to another round of hearings and markup sessions. Most bills that return to the full committee do make it to the floor of the chamber from which they came.

Once a bill returns to the floor of the House or Senate, it is in serious contention for actually becoming a law. But there are yet several hurdles to make before that happens. In the House, the flow of bills is regulated by the **Rules Committee.** This body decides when and under what terms a bill will be debated in the House. Under open rules, a bill can be amended on the floor. Under closed rules, no amendments are allowed. Under a modified closed rule, specific amendments may be allowed or certain sections of the bill may be amended. These rules can have a drastic effect on the chances for a bill's passage. They can also help to determine whether a bill resembles its original form after it passes and whether or not it has any real force. And, of course, how a bill is scheduled may determine whether it actually ever does reach the floor for debate.

Once the bill is before the House and the rules are established, the House uses a special parliamentary procedure that allows debate with a quorum of less than half of the representatives. It is called the **Committee of the Whole House,** and most legislation is debated in this way. Opposing sides take turns stating their cases, supporting or opposing the bill, introducing amendments, and supporting or opposing those. In the end a vote is taken and, usually, votes are recorded electronically. Voice votes are still used sometimes, however, and they allow members to vote more or less anonymously. If more than half of those voting say yes to the bill, it is on its way to the Senate.

Another parliamentary tool the House uses is called **suspension of the rules,** sometimes used for bills that are not controversial. The speaker may consider a motion for a suspension of the rules if a quorum is present and if there seems to be an urgent need to move the bill quickly. Passage of the bill under this condition requires an affirmative vote of two-thirds of members present. The procedure is uncommon.

Bills come to the Senate floor and are debated there in a very different fashion. While bills are normally debated in the order in which they appear, the majority leader working with the full consent of the Senate can move bills to the floor out of order. If both parties have agreed to the bill, it may be enacted by **unanimous consent,** usually by voice vote, with only a brief reading of its title and a request by the leadership that it be adopted without objection. If one or more members object, the bill will either be set aside or debated.

On the Senate floor, the ensuing debate has no limits. The leadership can request limits by calling for unanimous consent, but Senators can talk for as long as they want about any bill. If they are capable and willing, they may speak until a bill is beyond the point where it can be voted on. This is called **filibustering,** and it can be stopped only when a **cloture motion,** signed by at least sixteen senators, is filed. At that point, if two-thirds of the senators agree, the debate ends.

In the Senate there is no rules committee comparable to that of the House, but there is a procedure known as the **unanimous consent agreement.** If all senators agree to it, this arrangement puts limits on debate and on amendments to some bills and thus speeds them through the Senate.

Another controversial aspect of Senate action involves amendments, which can be offered after the first three hours of debate. They, too, are subject to unlimited debate. The amendments need not be relevant to the bills being considered. This has been used to get controversial measures passed by attaching them to unrelated and relatively innocuous bills and piggybacking them through the process.

Bills that make it through the House go to the Senate for action, and vice versa. Having made it through one chamber, the bill must go through the same process—subcommittee and committee action, floor debate, possible amendments, more debate—and gain the support of the majority of that second house before it moves on. From there, if it has survived, it goes to the president.

Sometimes two bills that are similar or identical are introduced in both houses. These are called **companion bills,** and by introducing them, sponsors have a greater chance of getting their proposed laws passed. If one companion bill dies, the other may survive. When both bills pass, they usually go to a **conference committee,** a group made up of members from both houses, where they are forged into one bill.

A conference committee might also be called to work on a bill that has been changed significantly in the second house that considers it. This committee's process is no different than that of any other committee. That is, the bill can be reworked to the point of being rewritten. It can still die at this point, if the conferees do not reach agreement. If they do agree, they issue a report describing their recommendations. But once the bill passes this stage, it must be approved without any changes by both houses before it can be sent to the president for signature or veto.

A bill in the president's office can become a law in two ways. The president can sign the bill into law or let it sit in the Oval Office for ten days without signing it. In the latter case, if Congress is still in session after those ten days, the bill automatically becomes a law. If Congress adjourns during that period, however, the bill dies a death known as a **pocket veto.**

If the president decides to veto a bill and Congress is still in session, the bill returns to Congress. Senators and representatives have an opportunity then to override the veto and make the bill a law. That requires a two-thirds vote in both houses.

The story of how a bill becomes a law—summarized in figure 4.1—plays out similarly in most state legislatures. Most governors have powers that extend beyond those of the president in their respective legislative processes. Almost all states give their governors the **line-item veto,** which allows them to veto parts of a bill while signing the rest of it into law. Some governors have the power to reduce amounts authorized within spending bills and others can add executive amendments to bills. These are recommended changes that make the bill acceptable to the governor, if the legislature adopts them on reconsidering the bill after the veto.

OPPORTUNITIES FOR INPUT

Citizens and interest groups can and do influence the legislative process. If you consider how a bill becomes a law, you can see several points at which this is possible. At other points it is not so obvious that the process can be influenced.

Citizens and interest groups can and do influence the legislative process.

Following the Bill

The first obvious opportunity for influence is at the origin of the bill. Anyone can get a bill drafted, if they can get the attention of a legislator and someone who knows how to do the drafting. Of course, that isn't as easy as it sounds. It helps to have the backing of a substantial organization—one with some political clout and a lawyer who can write the proposed bill in the proper way. Influencing the lawmaking process often means first playing politics within an organization, trying to get that organization to support a cause and get legislation drafted.

The next obvious step is to get a sponsor for the proposed legislation. This part can be difficult because legislators at all levels are usually extremely busy, and many people compete for their time and energy. While it is difficult, it is worth the effort, because getting a legislator to the point of sponsoring a bill means securing

Figure 4.1 Civics 101: An Overview of the Federal Legislative Process

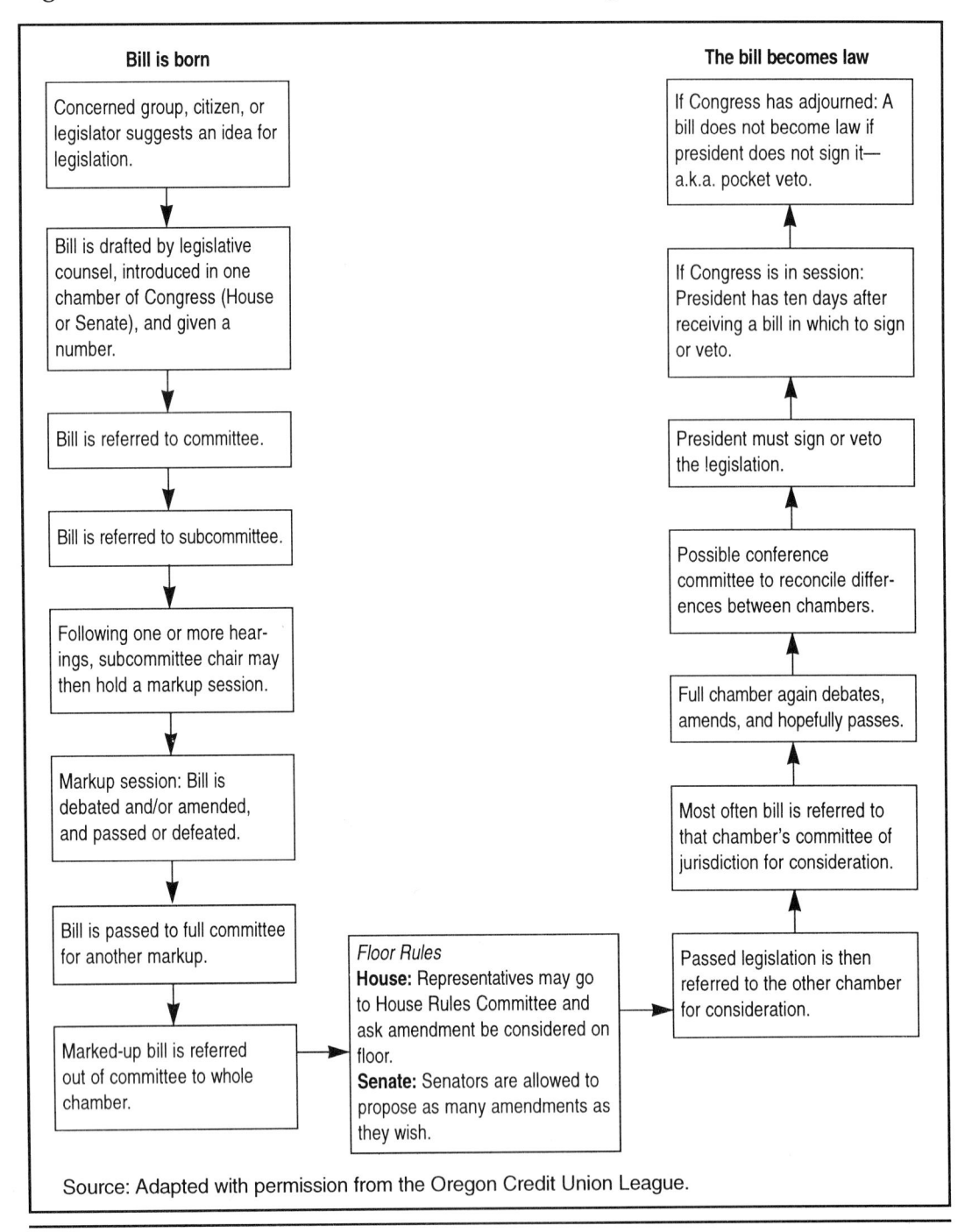

Bill is born

- Concerned group, citizen, or legislator suggests an idea for legislation.
- Bill is drafted by legislative counsel, introduced in one chamber of Congress (House or Senate), and given a number.
- Bill is referred to committee.
- Bill is referred to subcommittee.
- Following one or more hearings, subcommittee chair may then hold a markup session.
- Markup session: Bill is debated and/or amended, and passed or defeated.
- Bill is passed to full committee for another markup.
- Marked-up bill is referred out of committee to whole chamber.

Floor Rules
House: Representatives may go to House Rules Committee and ask amendment be considered on floor.
Senate: Senators are allowed to propose as many amendments as they wish.

The bill becomes law

- If Congress has adjourned: A bill does not become law if president does not sign it—a.k.a. pocket veto.
- If Congress is in session: President has ten days after receiving a bill in which to sign or veto.
- President must sign or veto the legislation.
- Possible conference committee to reconcile differences between chambers.
- Full chamber again debates, amends, and hopefully passes.
- Most often bill is referred to that chamber's committee of jurisdiction for consideration.
- Passed legislation is then referred to the other chamber for consideration.

Source: Adapted with permission from the Oregon Credit Union League.

44   *Chapter Four*

a solid commitment and getting the bill introduced. Legislators do not take sponsorship lightly. Again, it helps to have the backing of an organization with some political power.

Once a bill has a sponsor, an important next step is finding cosponsors. As with finding a sponsor, this can be challenging, but once a bill has a sponsor, you have at least one supporter to point to in seeking others. The more cosponsors you get, the more momentum you have, and the easier it is to get more. And cosponsors can keep signing on, right up to the day on which the vote is taken. For many organizations, this is a key step in gaining political influence over a piece of legislation. Organizations spend significant time, money, and energy getting representatives to sign on as cosponsors to proposed legislation. In the case of H.R. 1151, for example, supporters of the bill expended such an effort, and when the House vote was taken, the bill had 207 cosponsors from both parties.

Once a new bill is referred to its committee and subcommittee, the next place for people to make their preferences known is at the hearings held by those bodies. These hearings very seldom make the newspapers or the evening news. Furthermore, in order to testify you have to be invited by the committee. Those who testify are usually experts on the subject being discussed, or they have political prominence in the subject area. Each has a relatively short time—a few minutes or maybe hours—to try to make a direct impact on the lawmaking process.

Congressional committees are extremely busy and so are limited in terms of how many people can testify at their hearings. However, every U.S. citizen technically has the right to testify at most committee and subcommittee hearings. You can get yourself invited if you can prove to the committee or subcommittee that you have something significant to contribute. One way is to write a letter to the chair of the committee or subcommittee, demonstrating that you have the education, the knowledge, and the capability to testify in a meaningful manner. It is a good idea to send a copy of your letter to your representative and, even better, to have the support of that representative before sending the letter. That person might then be able to reinforce your efforts to be invited to testify.

In most state legislatures, on the other hand, it is not so difficult to appear before a committee or subcommittee. In a typical state legislature, most hearings are accessible to just about anyone who wants to testify. You need to show up well before the time of the hearing, sign a list, and then wait your turn. Of course, a limited number of people can testify, but most people are limited only by whether or not they get to the meeting room early enough to sign the list.

Lobbying

Most people never get to testify at legislative hearings, but they can still have influence in two major ways—through **lobbying** and through **grassroots activities. Direct lobbying** involves paying someone to attend the process nearly full time, to seek access to lawmakers, and to spend time convincing them of certain views. Grassroots work, sometimes called **grassroots lobbying,** is less direct and less expensive, but it can involve a lot more work by a lot more people.

Most people can still have influence in two major ways—through lobbying and through grassroots activities.

Frequently, the amount of attention a committee member will pay to a given bill is determined by how important it seems to his or her constituents, and grassroots lobbying efforts can make a difference. Opponents and supporters of legislation on which hearings are being held can call and write to their appropriate representatives to make their views known. They can also send faxes and e-mail, and as technology continues to develop, they will probably have more ways to communicate their views.

Ironically, with all of the available communication modes, the most effective one is probably still the old-fashioned handwritten letter. It carries more weight—literally and figuratively—than a voice on the phone or electrons moving from one computer to another. It is tangible evidence, something that has obviously taken some effort on the part of its sender, and it is more likely to get the attention of the recipient. Printed letters and faxes are almost as effective, although clearly less personal than handwritten messages. Phone calls and e-mail can get the message across, but they can more easily get lost before they get heard or read. In fact, some legislators' assistants say that a letter is more likely than e-mail to get to the intended recipient. Low technology, in this case, is more reliable.

Grassroots lobbyists also try to amplify their messages by convincing acquaintances, groups, and organizations to call their representatives. This might mean sending literature alerting group members to make their views known and to tell others to do the same. It can also mean circulating petitions, writing letters to the editor, calling for meetings with congressional representatives, and contributing to campaign funds. What gets said and heard in committee hearings sometimes reflects a well-organized grassroots campaign.

Lobbying is a more immediate way of trying to influence the legislative process. The first people to be known as lobbyists were Englishmen of the seventeenth century who waited in the large lobby adjacent to the House of Commons, where they hoped to speak directly with members of Parliament. Lobbyists of our day are more likely to be found in hotel lobbies and in waiting rooms outside the offices of legislators. And they are no longer only men. Every year, more women become lobbyists and heads of lobbying firms. Any interest group can send a lobbyist to Washington, D.C., or to a state capitol, where they do essentially the same work as their English counterparts did three hundred years ago.

Lobbyists and many of the interest groups they represent have come to be resented by a large share of the American public. Many people fear that democracy is being destroyed or at least threatened by special interests and their "hired guns." The call for reform legislation has been loud and clear. In response, Congress has passed laws designed to make lobbyists and legislators more accountable and to control any underhanded aspects of lobbying. We took a quick look at this legislation in chapter 3 while considering the rules of the election game. We take a closer look here.

The Current Rules

The **Lobbying Disclosure Act of 1995** was passed to strengthen the rules in force under the Federal Regulation of Lobbying Act of 1946. It uses a broader definition of "lobbyist" and requires more in the way of disclosure by lobbyists of their activities. Whereas the old law was limited to lobbying of members of Congress, the 1995 act covers lobbying of members of Congress, their staff members, and most officials of the executive branch. Under the old law, only lobbyists who spent a majority of their time lobbying had to register with the government. As of 1995, anyone spending more than 20 percent of their time as a lobbyist must register. And where foreign lobbyists were exempted from the rules under the old law, they must now register and obey the rules like everyone else.

The disclosure rules are also more stringent now. Anyone receiving more than $5,000 in a six-month period as pay for lobbying must file two reports per year with Congress. The same goes for organizations that spend more than $20,000 on lobbying within a six-month period. Each report must include the issues on which the lobbyist is working, specific bills being discussed, the executive agency or house of Congress being lobbied, the identity of the organization paying the lobbyist, and the approximate cost of the reported lobbying efforts.

The 1995 law does not cover grassroots lobbying campaigns, no matter who orchestrates them. Nor does it cover tax-exempt organizations like churches. Also, the semiannual reports that lobbyists file do not have to identify specific individuals approached by lobbyists. Some critics have found these to be significant shortcomings. The most cynical of detractors have questioned how tough the law can be when it was written, or at least influenced by, the people it's supposed to be regulating—members of Congress and lobbyists. Be that as it may, there are penalties for violation of the rules of the 1995 act. Those who fail to abide by the rules are subject to fines of up to $50,000.

States, too, have enacted laws to regulate lobbying. Many are similar to the federal law; some are much more strict. Minnesota, for example, requires lobbyists to report on any expenditures of $5 or more in value. The state's legislators cannot accept gifts of any kind from lobbyists, and that includes picking up the tab at lunch or dinner.

While many people suspect that lobbying is nothing more than a method of buying votes, the great majority of lobbyists avoid outright bribery. Instead, their most important goal is to build relationships. The smart lobbyist realizes that legislators are busy people with multiple issues to keep informed about and plenty of work to do. Even the legislators' staffs are strained in managing the load of information that descends on them. Lobbyists help out by providing key data, fact sheets, summaries of important studies, public opinion information, and even speeches that legislators can use to support or oppose a bill. They also provide information that can be inserted in the **Congressional Record** on behalf of the representative with whom they are dealing. All of this assistance is highly valuable.

Smart lobbyists also identify their allies in the legislative process, and spend time and resources on those people and on legislators who are undecided on their issue. They avoid wasting resources on legislators who are entrenched in opposition to their causes. In this way—by building relationships and alliances—lobbyists and their interest groups can gain influence in the legislative process. As legislators and their staffs come to rely on lobbyists for valuable information and assistance, lobbyists might even get involved in drafting bills, planning hearings, and campaigning among undecided legislators, more or less on behalf of the legislators with whom they have built relationships.

How to Stay Tuned—Tools for Political Action

Lobbying and grassroots work can play a big role all the way through the legislative process. The markup session, which follows the hearing stage, is an especially important phase. After each hearing, a transcript is printed and distributed to committee members and is available in the Congressional Record. Those concerned about what happens to legislation need to be vigilant at this point. And participation by committee members is crucial, because much can happen and each member can have a lot to say about what happens. What their constituents and lobbyists say and do can make a difference in whether and how they participate.

To have influence, citizens and groups need to pay close attention, not only to hearing transcripts and markup sessions, but also to subsequent committee work and to floor debates in both houses. There are various ways to learn about the schedules and records of what is going on in Congress. To get general information over the phone, you can call the Clerk of the House at (202)226-5200. The place to call for Senate information is the Secretary of the Senate at (202)224-2115. In every state there are similar information offices for the legislative houses. You can look in the phone book, give them a call, and find out what is scheduled, what is happening, and what has already happened.

> *To have influence, citizens and groups need to pay close attention.*

In Washington, D.C., anyone can visit the official repository of all published documents of the House and its committees. They are stored in the **Legislative Resource Center (LRC)** operated by the Office of the Clerk of the House. In addition, the LRC contains the lobbyist registration lists and the disclosure reports that lobbyists must file. It also is a place where lobbyists can register. You can reach or visit the LRC using the information in figure 4.2.

The Legislative Process 49

Figure 4.2 Reaching the LRC

Mailing address:	Legislative Resource Center B106 Cannon House Office Building Washington, D.C. 20515–6612
Phone number:	(202) 226–5200
E-mail (general):	LRC @ clerk.house.gov
E-mail (documents):	Hdocs @ clerk.house.gov
E-mail (archives):	Archives @ clerk.house.gov
Office hours:	9:00-6:00 Monday–Friday

(House documents available also when House is in session.)

An invaluable tool is the Congressional Record, which is exactly what its name implies. Every day of every session, reporters work in ten-minute shifts, recording all proceedings. By the following morning, all of those notes, plus supporting documents and inserts offered by members of Congress, are printed in the Congressional Record. It is available in some libraries, although they usually receive it on a periodic basis.

The Congressional Record is a relatively low-technology option for keeping up with the legislative process, and not everyone can travel to Washington, D.C., to visit the LRC. But there are other excellent options. Since 1986, the nonprofit **Cable Satellite Public Affairs Network (C-SPAN)** has offered live television and radio coverage of floor proceedings in both houses. C-SPAN and now C-SPAN2 have expanded their offerings and cover committee hearings, speeches, and other events pertinent to the working of our government.

Probably the best tool is a connection to the Internet. It offers a wealth of information, sometimes very close to real-time, on events in Washington, D.C., as well as in the state capitols. Using sites like *Congress.org* and *Thomas.gov* you can get the text of the Congressional Record right on your computer screen. You can read House and Senate floor schedules, see what committees are meeting, and even read hearing testimony. Most committees and subcommittees now have web sites.

And most sites have plenty of links to keep you surfing for as long as you want. Figure 4.3 lists and describes outstanding web sites.

Most committees and subcommittees now have web sites.

The newer and faster technology can be important to you if you want to keep up, because some bills move faster than others. While most lawmaking is a slow and grinding process, some bills are sped through, and, unfortunately, some are actually sneaked through. Those who are on top of the situation have the most to say about what those bills look like when they emerge. A lot can be gained or lost in a short period of time.

To have influence, citizens and groups not only have to stay informed. They also need to let their representatives on the committees and subcommittees know exactly what they want from them, and again, they must not lose time in doing so. The reason this can make a difference is that legislators do not always know how to vote on all the issues. Sometimes it is very clear to them how to vote. Some votes are obvious party-line votes, for example. Others are massively supported by almost all constituents. Still others involve issues on which the representatives have consistently taken strong stands.

But some votes are not so clear-cut. For example, they might deal with issues that are very complex and on which the public is sharply divided. There are cases in which most constituents are relatively uninformed and have given no clear consensus. And there are certainly instances when the representatives themselves have not been able to comprehend the details. In those cases, representatives welcome strong signals from citizens and groups.

When we hear about grassroots campaigns and lobbying, we usually think about legislatures. But the executive branch of government is another place where these efforts can make a difference. While it would be difficult to get much time

Figure 4.3 Outstanding Web Sites

The World Wide Web contains numerous sites that provide useful information for those who want to be informed about politics and government. As of this writing, the following sites are particularly good for information on the legislative process.

- **Congress.org** (http://policy.net/capweb/congress.html) contains excellent features, including a congressional directory by alphabetic listing and by state and information on House and Senate committees and on the leadership offices. You can find your members by typing in your ZIP code. "Connecting with Congress" contains brief but useful descriptions of the legislative process and the congressional staff, information on visiting Capitol Hill, and tips on writing to members. "Congress Today" includes schedules for the day in both houses and committee hearing schedules for the week, complete with meeting room numbers. And you can e-mail anyone in Congress from this site.

- **Library of Congress** (http://www.loc.gov) contains "documents, photographs, movies and sound recordings that tell America's story." This site has a wealth of historical information and very useful research and education tools. One of those tools is a web site called "Thomas" that was created "in the spirit of Thomas Jefferson."

- **Thomas** (http://thomas.loc.gov) gives full access to bills and resolutions under consideration in Congress, recent and upcoming House and Senate floor activities, summaries of bills, texts of bills, status reports on key bills, and records of House and Senate votes. Other features include the text and index of the Congressional Record, House and Senate directories, and committee information (reports, schedules, and home-page links). For background information, you can click on a detailed description of the legislative process and on historical documents such as the Declaration of Independence and the Federalist Papers.

Figure 4.3 Outstanding Web Sites *(continued)*

- **House of Representatives Home Page** (http://www.house.gov) is a straightforward posting of a wide variety of basic information such as the annual legislative schedule, information on bills being considered, current schedule for the House floor, committee hearing schedules, reports on "current events," and the voting records of the representatives. It also has lots of links to education sites, tourist information, and other government sites, plus home pages for each representative, most committees, and the leadership offices. Finally, it includes a House Directory.

- **Senate Home Page** (http://www.senate.gov) is very similar to the House home page, containing most of the features of that site, plus some interesting historical information.

- **Office of the Clerk of the House** (http://clerkweb.house.gov) contains information on the Legislative Resource Center and other services of the Office of the Clerk.

and attention from the president and most governors, executive agencies hear every day from interest groups of all kinds. These agencies, such as the NCUA, make the rules that put teeth into laws.

Although rules are somewhat dictated by the laws, there is a rule-making process that has some of the same elements of lawmaking. Agencies often hold public hearings or call for public comments to get information and feedback on rules that already exist and rules that are being considered. What they hear in this process can have a big impact on the final outcome. Agency heads and managers also pay attention to public opinion as reflected in what they hear and read in the papers. They, in turn, have obviously strong influence over how the agencies function in applying the law. So players in the political game cannot afford to stop paying attention, once a bill is signed by the president or a governor.

RELATIONSHIP BETWEEN ELECTIONS AND LAWMAKING

Our representatives are our **delegates.** We have delegated to them the work of government. We are their **constituents.** Together, within each district, we constitute their reason for going to work. Put more simply, they work for us. In theory it is that simple; in practice it is not.

Our legislators and executive employees are physically far removed from most of us. We can't keep an eye on them as most bosses can with employees in their places of work. The workings of politics and government are beyond most of us. They are incredibly complex and are growing more so every year. Even if we could observe our government representatives at work, most of us couldn't always tell if they were doing a good job or not.

Fortunately, there are people among us, such as scholars and journalists, who take on the roles of watching and reporting on the work of our government. But even they are hard put to stay on top of everything that happens in Washington, D.C., and in Raleigh and Austin and Sacramento and St. Paul. Ultimately, we have to judge the performance of our government employees and we have to decide whether they should keep working for us or not.

There are people who take on the roles of watching and reporting on the work of our government.

Our representatives, at the very least, must heed what we as their constituents say. While the level of respect and sympathy for politicians has suffered over the years, the fact is that heeding constituents is a hard job. Our legislators each represent a diverse group of people with sharply differing interests. They must weigh the preferences of the majority against the needs of minorities. To function effectively from day to day, they must factor in pressures from party members and, to some extent, satisfy a minimal number of campaign contributors. And they must heed their own best judgment and their consciences.

Considering all of these factors, they must plot a course that will allow them to get their jobs done and to maintain enough voter support to keep getting reelected. Of course, the more they get reelected, the more confidence, power, and latitude they gain in their decision making as they do their jobs. But as many former politicians can attest, one is never guaranteed a job for life as a representative of citizens of the United States.

All these forces acting together determine how legislators vote and how laws get made. The complexity of it can be overwhelming. It is no wonder that there is an entire scholarly discipline—political science—devoted to figuring it all out. Not even the best political scientists can come up with a formula to predict how any legislator will vote on any particular bill. However, as our system has evolved, it is safe to say that it still relies on one fundamental relationship. That is, as long as we are a nation of laws as described by our Constitution, there will be elections. And as long as there are elections, legislators will need to heed their constituents in the process of making laws.

CHAPTER FIVE

CREDIT UNIONS IN THE ELECTION PROCESS

With a fundamental understanding of the election and legislative processes from the last two chapters, the challenge will be to translate that understanding into results for your credit union. After all, it doesn't do you any good to understand the process if you can't make it work for the benefit of your credit union and its members. The rest of this handbook will focus on the roles available to you in the election and legislative processes to further your impact on the people that can decide the credit union's future. The first step in having an impact is to establish, maintain, and develop a connection with your credit union's legislators.

The first step is to establish, maintain, and develop a connection with your credit union's legislators.

IMPORTANCE OF RELATIONSHIP BUILDING

The Oregon League has retained Ted Hughes as its outside lobbyist since the early 1970s. He's recognized as one of the deans of lobbyists around Oregon's state capitol, someone who knows how the game of politics is really played. When Ted's giving speeches to groups about the legislative process, he likes to tell them, "Every legislator has three priorities once he's elected, and it's the same three for every legislator. First, he's going to help the people that got him elected. Second, he's going to help the people that got him elected. And, third, he's going to help the people that got him elected."

It's natural for a politician's mentality to run along these lines. Generally, each can identify just a few interest groups, neighborhoods, or demographics that were principally responsible for his or her election, and that politician will work hardest to ensure that their interests are protected.

After all, most politicians get started in politics because there is a particular issue that captures their passion or interest. How many local legislators can you think of who started out being identified with one particular issue or interest group? They work with groups that share that passion or interest to carry it forward. At some point, they perhaps recognize that they can better affect change for that issue from inside the halls of Congress or the state legislature, so they make their bid for public office.

Once they decide to take the plunge, whom do they turn to for their initial support, guidance, and contributions but that same special interest group that pulled them into the process to begin with. Once they're elected, they pursue that issue or agenda as a legislator because that topic holds some special interest for them. And you can bet that their top priorities will be protecting the interests of the people who first banded together to lend them support for their run for office.

Our goal in affecting change for credit unions in the political arena is to become involved in these campaigns at the earliest possible stages. We need to be recognized as a group that was influential in the election of a politician for that person to be willing to pay attention to our priorities once elected. After all, as Ted Hughes is also fond of pointing out, once a politician is elected to office, his or her real job is to make sure to get reelected the next time out.

> *Our goal is to become involved in these campaigns at the earliest possible stages.*

So your credit union's first goal in getting involved in the election process should be to identify **opportunity races**—those elections in which getting involved can really make a difference. Entrenched candidates with established support groups and token opposition have little incentive to tackle potentially divisive issues like those surrounding credit unions. The races in which credit union involvement and support can make a difference should be the ones to which we dedicate the bulk of our efforts and resources.

Strong relationships with leaders in the legislative process provide you access to them at a crucial point. That access then allows you to emphasize your point of view and have it be viewed as credible, and it generally opens the channels of communication between you and legislative leaders to make sure your interests are advanced or protected, as need be.

The 1998 efforts in Congress through the Campaign for Consumer Choice provide an excellent case study. On April 1, 1998, H.R. 1151, the Credit Union Access Act, passed the House of Representatives by a vote of 411 to 8. This overwhelming success was the culmination of more than a year of grassroots lobbying efforts by credit unions across the country. But one relationship with one legislator had more to do with ensuring that success than any other. Speaker of the House Newt Gingrich is a staunch credit union supporter. He used his influence as the leader of the House to shepherd H.R. 1151 to adoption, pushing and prodding behind the scenes to bring the bill out of the House Banking Committee and to the full House floor for an opportunity to pass overwhelmingly.

Why did the leader of the House make H.R. 1151 his priority and use his considerable influence to ensure its passage? Speaker Gingrich has a long-standing relationship with credit unions in Georgia (his home state), which have taken an active role in his election campaigns. Figure 5.1 lists the credit union activities that the Georgia League has coordinated over the years to build and maintain this relationship.

The important lessons to be learned from this experience are twofold. First, it shows how success in the legislative process hinges on your relationship with legislative leaders. Speaker Gingrich's dedication to the passage of H.R. 1151 virtually guaranteed its swift consideration from the date of the Supreme Court's decision in late February to House passage on April 1, a remarkably swift journey through our usually stilted processes.

Second, and most important, it shows how early and intensely Georgia credit unions got involved in Gingrich's congressional campaigns. Did they know he was going to be Speaker someday? No one could have predicted that development back when their involvement began. The Georgia credit unions just knew how important it was to build a relationship with their congressional representatives. Luckily for the entire credit union movement, they did such a good job that Speaker Gingrich was ready to help them when they (and we all) needed it.

Who will be the next Speaker of the House? Who will chair your legislature's banking committee next session? No one knows the answers to these questions now, but we *do* know that unless we get involved in building relationships with

Figure 5.1 The Steps to Building a Relationship with a Legislator

> **A Historical Review of the Georgia Credit Union Movement's Involvement with Speaker of the House Newt Gingrich**
>
> **1990** In the fall, league staff organized a phone bank one week prior to the election (a technique they'd pioneered for credit unions with Representative Doug Barnard's campaign).
>
> **1991** Staff attend town hall meetings, maintain contact (although minimal) with Gingrich's campaign and congressional staff.
>
> **1992** Gingrich's district is restructured after the 1990 census. Facing a difficult challenge in this new legislative district, Georgia credit unions recognize the opportunity to forge a strong link by taking an early and intense involvement in the campaign. Gingrich toured the league offices and met with key management and staff. He toured four credit unions in his district and held a lunch with women professionals from credit unions in his new district. Credit unions sponsored an ice cream social for Representative Gingrich to meet his constituents.
>
> **1993** Gingrich is elected minority whip and speaks at CUNA's Governmental Affairs Conference as well as the Georgia League's annual meeting. Credit union representatives attend numerous fund-raisers, including Gingrich's fiftieth birthday party (where they were lucky enough to sit with Gingrich's wife).
>
> **1994** Credit union support continues with direct monetary contributions to Gingrich's campaign and attending numerous fund-raisers. League staff coordinate congressional office visits, including delivering authentic Georgia barbeque for lunch during hill visits, through Gingrich's office. That arrangement allowed for a constant working relationship with Gingrich's staff.
>
> **1995** Gingrich is elected Speaker of the House in January after the Republican Party unexpectedly assumed control of the House after the 1994 elections. In June, Georgia credit unions host a reception in Gingrich's honor. Although scheduled for 200 people, more than 430 attended, drawing national, local, and credit union media coverage.
>
> **1996** On one day's notice, arranged for forty-three credit union people to work at Gingrich's campaign office to coordinate a campaign mailing.

Figure 5.1 The Steps to Building a Relationship with a Legislator *(continued)*

1997 Speaker Gingrich consulted with CUNA and Georgia League staff on strategy for introduction of the Credit Union Access Act (H.R. 1151). Credit union people continue to show up at Gingrich's campaign events, including thirty-six credit union supporters attending a quarterly "Business Leaders" breakfast (out of a total attendance of 150); assisting with campaign office duties like folding and labeling over eight thousand invitations to Gingrich's birthday party celebration; and conducting a phone bank to reach over twenty-four hundred people. Three hundred six credit union supporters end up attending the party (out of a total crowd of twenty-five hundred); credit union attendees are easily identified wearing credit union logo shirts.

Involvement continued with campaign and congressional activities during the summer, including raising money for a Habitat for Humanity house built through a "Women for Newt" campaign group. The group requested credit unions to contribute $5,000 as a sponsor of the event; they raised $14,100. On the day credit union people were to help on the Habitat house, sixty-seven people turned up to work on the project and were served lunch by Speaker Gingrich.

In conjunction with CUNA, the Georgia League held a fund-raiser for Speaker Gingrich in Washington, D.C. and raised over $50,000 for his reelection campaign. Credit unions were recognized by the Speaker during a Habitat for Humanity dedication at the Capitol for their hard work.

1998 Speaker Gingrich is keynote speaker at CUNA's Governmental Affairs Conference, where he announces his cosponsorship of H.R. 1151. Credit unions commit to the Speaker's "House that Congress Built" Habitat project by working two out of the eight weeks scheduled. In late April, over sixty credit union people spent the day working with the Speaker and some of his staff on the Habitat House.

Other Steps Georgia Credit Unions Took:
- Attended town hall meetings whenever possible to make sure that Speaker Gingrich saw familiar faces and made the connection with credit unions and his congressional activities.

Figure 5.1 The Steps to Building a Relationship with a Legislator *(continued)*

- Made sure key people were at public events attended by the Speaker. Showed an interest in activities outside of just credit union issues; tried to support the Speaker's other interests and causes so the Speaker knew credit union people were active in many areas of the community.
- Made an effort to come through in the tough times and deliver promises. Georgia credit union people drove two and a half hours to attend a fund-raiser in South Carolina that they knew the Speaker would attend. Such dedication really stood out. Many of the campaign activities were last-minute, desperate events where the credit unions made a tremendous impression by getting the people together to get the job done, whatever it was. Coming through in the clutch gets you noticed and appreciated.

Special thanks to Cindy Connelly, Senior Vice-President, Georgia Credit Union Affiliates.

our state and federal legislators, we won't be in a position to succeed when the next credit union issue arises. So the balance of this chapter will explain what you can do to develop that sort of relationship with your legislators.

POLITICAL CONTRIBUTIONS

In our political system it's almost impossible to be elected to any legislative office without raising and spending a lot of money. Even local state legislator races carry campaign budgets over six figures, and million-dollar campaigns for local offices are not unheard of. In chapter 3, we reviewed the campaign process and the importance of money in that process. While we can never match our political opponents dollar-for-dollar in money raised or spent, we still can raise and contribute significant campaign dollars if we use all our resources wisely. Let's explore the various avenues available to credit unions to raise money for political campaigns.

We still can raise and contribute significant campaign dollars if we use all our resources wisely.

Political Action Committees (PACs)

PACs are the frontline supplier of funds for most political campaigns. Generally, PACs are organized around a particular special interest or business group. For example, the **Credit Union Legislative Action Council (CULAC)** was organized by CUNA to contribute funds in federal races to candidates that support credit unions and their issues. CULAC is a federally registered PAC that must comply with the strictures and limitations established by the Federal Election Commission.

Your state league may have also organized its own federal PAC, and other credit union groups have also formed their own PACs to support their narrower agendas. Remember the discussion about permission agreements from chapter 3—your credit union can only allow one federal PAC focused on credit union issues to solicit contributions from its volunteers, employees, and members in a calendar year. So if you have already given CULAC permission to solicit through your credit union, you cannot give permission to your state league for its federal PAC or for any other credit union trade association PAC.

However, your state league may have organized a state PAC to assist candidates for state elective offices. Those state PACs are governed by state laws. Signing a permission agreement or contributing to CULAC does not prevent or in any real way limit your credit union from also supporting your league's state-level political activities. Contribution and expenditure limitations and requirements for those state PACs usually differ substantially from those governing federal PACs like CULAC, so check with your state league for further guidelines on their PACs.

CULAC is funded entirely by contributions from individuals—personal checks and cash donations by credit union volunteers, employees, and members, as well as contributions from league and CUNA volunteers and staff. Increasingly, CULAC is becoming recognized as the leading player in credit union-related political campaign issues. But funding for CULAC will have to be increased substantially before it can provide any meaningful contrast to the millions of dollars raised and spent by the bankers and our other political opponents. That's why our challenge, as you'll see later in this chapter, is to use our advantages in other areas of the election process to counteract the dollar impact that bankers can generate.

Credit Unions

Federal credit unions are prohibited by federal law from making direct contributions of any kind to political candidates or campaigns. For more specific guidance on allowable activities for federal credit unions, refer to the following authorities, copies of which are included in the appendix to this handbook:

- NCUA Interpretive Ruling and Policy Statement (IRPS) 79-6 dated July 10, 1979;
- NCUA General Counsel Opinion Letter 92-0613 dated June 17, 1992;
- NCUA General Counsel Opinion Letter 92-1202 dated March 3, 1993;

Copies of these and other research resources are also available through NCUA's web site at www.ncua.gov.

In basic terms, the permissible political activities for a federal credit union are limited. Individual credit union volunteers, management, and staff can and should be encouraged to contribute to candidates and PACs on their own behalf. Also, a federal credit union can engage in direct education efforts to its members, encouraging them to contribute to and support particular candidates or PACs. These options will be discussed more fully later in this chapter.

State credit unions may have a number of options for direct participation in the political process, depending on each credit union's state laws. The first option state credit unions may have is to contribute directly to state and local candidate campaigns. Generally, all corporate contributions are prohibited in federal elections, except for soft money contributions to political parties. Given our earlier discussion about credit unions remaining nonpartisan, direct contributions to political parties are usually discouraged.

The second option is for state credit unions to make direct contributions to state league PACs, so long as state election law allows corporate contributions to state PACs. Both of these options carry a consequence, however.

Any contribution from state credit unions to a political candidate or a state PAC that makes candidate contributions would be subject to a 35 percent federal income tax. Political contributions made by nonprofit corporations like credit unions, if made to a candidate or a PAC that supports candidates, trigger the requirement for the state credit union to file an IRS Form 1120-POL for the calendar year in which that contribution was made. Such contributions may also trigger state tax consequences.

Staff and Volunteers

Credit union staff and volunteers for both state and federal credit unions should be encouraged to participate in the legislative process by making direct contributions to credit union PACs and political candidates. If you understand that federal PACs like CULAC can only be funded by individual contributions, where better to search for those contributors than with the people who devote their spare time or their profession to credit unions? Those people in leadership roles in your credit union should demonstrate their commitment to protecting and advancing the movement by making contributions and encouraging everyone to participate.

Of course, contributions must and should remain voluntary by each individual. But properly educated and motivated credit union staff and volunteers could prove to be a great source for political action dollars. And the contributions by each person don't have to be large. If every volunteer and staff member in the over eleven thousand credit unions in the United States contributed $10 each and every year, CULAC funds would at least triple.

In encouraging participation, however, be careful not to run afoul of the contribution limitations. Remember, corporations cannot contribute to federal candidates, and they suffer tax consequences if contributing to state candidates, if it's allowed. **Pass-through arrangements**—individual volunteers or professionals make political contributions and then are "reimbursed" by the credit union for "expenses" or other false charges—clearly constitute an effort to skirt these limitations and expose the credit union to serious potential liability for evading election or taxation laws.

Members

The final, often overlooked source of funds for political contributions is your credit union's members. After all, they also are important stakeholders in preserving credit unions as a viable choice for financial institutions. Back in 1993, Multco Employees Credit Union in Portland, Oregon, decided to develop a direct approach to solicit credit union members for their support of the credit union's political action efforts.

The idea was developed by Bob Burns, Multco's manager, and he worked with representatives from CUNA and the Oregon League to develop the program and obtain the necessary regulatory approvals. Simply structured, Multco solicits

its members to contribute a flat dollar amount (usually $1 or $2) every month or quarter to support credit union political action. Periodically, the credit union sweeps the accounts and sends the contributions on to the CULAC and the Oregon state PAC.

The program was expanded by the Michigan League and, in light of the efforts of the Campaign for Consumer Choice, has gained even greater interest. CUNA has termed it the "Deduct-a-Buck Program" and has materials available to help credit unions start such a program with their members. If you thought $10 from every credit union volunteer and staff member would raise significant PAC contributions, how about just the average of $1 each year from the seventy-two million credit union members in the United States? That would really allow credit union issues to take prominence in the election process.

Credit Union PACs in the Election Process

Making a personal commitment to support credit union candidates with your own money, or your credit union's dollars if your state law allows it, certainly must raise your level of interest in how those dollars are invested. If you have contributed to CULAC or your league's state PAC, you have a right to know how those funds are allocated and who makes those decisions.

First, you must recognize that credit union PACs must make their decisions about whom to support based solely on a candidate's position on the issue of credit unions. Remember, the credit union approach is nonpartisan, so the PAC won't make contributions along political party lines. Also, our membership is too diverse to allow other issues to enter into our candidate evaluations. If we were to start asking candidates questions not only about their position on credit union issues but also on the environment, gun control, or prayer in school, we'd have a hard time coming to a consensus on whom to support. The scope of inquiry for any candidate should be limited to his or her position on issues that have a direct and important impact on credit unions.

How Decisions Are Made

Every PAC enters the election season with a daunting task of gathering as much pertinent information as possible about the entire field of candidates. At the federal level alone, over 465 races are contested every two years. Throw in the primaries, when states typically carry multiple candidates vying for their party's nomination, and you glimpse the daunting task that CUNA assumes in deciding to play in the federal election game. State PACs typically must make hundreds of their own decisions each election, depending on the size of their legislatures and how often they are elected. And don't think that you won't have an opportunity to participate in every race. Candidates at all levels are especially astute at finding out which organizations have active PACs and aren't shy about soliciting contributions.

The best way to ensure effective use of PAC dollars is to put them behind candidates who (1) support credit unions and (2) will win their races. You find out who supports credit unions by getting to know the candidates as well as you can. Determining who will win a race is much harder to learn and usually involves working with professionals at CUNA or the state league who engage in detailed research on demographics, party registrations, and voting histories. You would have to be pretty well connected in your local political scene to have much direct information about which candidate has the best chance to win. If you fit that mold, don't be shy about sharing that expertise with your league. However, even the most politically naive person can play a very active role in gathering as much information as possible about a candidate's position on credit unions.

Unless a candidate has a direct prior connection with credit unions (a former board or committee member, for example), he or she isn't likely to know much about our unique structure, our not-for-profit status, or current legislative issues involving credit unions. Election time is the perfect time to educate a candidate about credit unions: their role in the community, the important services they provide their members, and the types of support they make available to candidates who support their political agenda.

You have a great story to tell about how your credit union has made a positive impact on the lives and economic well-being of your members.

Your credit union should play a key role in that candidate's education. Face it, you have a great story to tell about how your credit union has made a positive impact on the lives and economic well-being of your members. Here's a list of possible activities to get that story across:

- Arrange a tour of your credit union for a candidate whom your league has identified in a key race in your district. Let the candidate see your operations and take the opportunity to explore the credit union difference. That's the best way for candidates to realize that we're a unique financial institution with a different political agenda.
- Invite the candidate to a reception with your volunteers and staff. If you have certain members or someone with the credit union who has been politically active, draw the candidate to that connection by having those persons at the reception and make a point of introducing them.
- Host a candidate night at your credit union where members can come and meet candidates for the contested races in your credit union's district. Give the candidates an opportunity to address credit union members about their concerns and the issues they see as important in the upcoming races.

Delivering PAC Contributions to Candidates

Of course, one way to attract a candidate's attention is to deliver a PAC contribution on behalf of CULAC or the state league. After all, if the credit union movement has decided to support a candidate, the worst way to express that support is by just mailing a check. Delivering contributions is yet another opportunity to forge or further that personal connection between a candidate and credit unions that helps foster a champion in the political arena.

If a PAC has decided to support a particular candidate, it is usually looking for someone in that candidate's district to deliver that check. Hopefully, you've already taken the steps of meeting the candidate, educating the candidate about credit unions and our issues, and playing an active role in building that relationship. When it comes time to deliver a PAC check, take the relationship to the next level. If you thought you had a candidate's attention when he or she was soliciting the contribution, imagine how much more interested the candidate will be in your issues now that you've made a commitment to support the election.

Either in tandem with someone from the league or on your own, make a special appointment to deliver the PAC check to the candidate. Take the opportunity to reinforce your earlier messages about credit unions and the issues coming up in the next session. Offer to provide the candidate with additional campaign assistance along the lines we'll discuss later in this chapter. One credit union manager even included a small personal contribution to the candidate with the PAC check. Some candidates would routinely accept the PAC check but then be genuinely impressed by the commitment the manager showed by including a personal contribution. (Of course, it was added incentive for the candidate to make the scheduled appointment, for if the candidate didn't show up, the manager would withhold the personal contribution check!) Use imaginative ways to stand out from the crowd and make the candidate's total experience with credit unions memorable.

Another way to maximize contributions and PAC resources is to use dedicated contributions for candidate events. Which do you think would make a bigger impact on a candidate: a $500 PAC check or a reception at the credit union where the candidate can meet dozens of credit union members whom you've invited specially to the event (and promised free snacks and soft drinks, so you're sure they'll show up)? Think you can throw a pretty impressive gathering for $500? Won't a candidate be more interested and focused if you help that person reach dozens of potential voters in one brief visit rather than just mingling your contribution with about a dozen others to buy one decent newspaper ad?

The types of events and receptions that attract candidates and allow them to connect with potential voters like your members or the general public are only limited by your imagination. Again, make your credit union something special in a candidate's experience, and you'll stand out months later when he or she is contacted by you about an important credit union issue.

Individual Credit Union PACs

Some credit unions have even established their own PACs to contribute to state candidates. Strategically, these credit union PACs allow multiple scenarios to promote and support election activities. For example, if your state has contribution limits, setting up individual credit union PACs might be a way to channel more contributions to good credit union supporters. Another scenario would be when your state league is faced with a difficult race in which more than one candidate is a strong credit union supporter. The league can support one of the candidates and coordinate support with the credit union's PAC to support the other good candidate in that race. That way, a relationship is developed but neither PAC is compromised by having contributed to both sides in the race. Contributing to both sides is usually a bad political tactic since it shows a lack of fortitude. You'll be asking politicians to make tough decisions to support you if contentious issues are raised; you should be willing to make an equally difficult decision about whom to support in the race.

Starting a PAC for your credit union is a difficult decision. You need to make sure you're ready to make a substantial enough commitment to support the complex recordkeeping and reporting that PAC administration requires. You'll need to raise enough money to make significant contributions in the races for districts where your credit union operates. Above all, make sure your PAC acts in concert with the league PAC's efforts to ensure that credit unions receive maximum impact for their political contribution dollars. You don't want the two PACs to operate at cross purposes and negate each other's influence. Credit unions can't afford to waste the money they invest in the political process.

IN-KIND CONTRIBUTIONS

Money is important to political campaigns, but it's not the only resource they need. Think like a campaign manager for a minute. Your goal is to communicate your candidate's message to the broadest number of potential voters for the least cost. Now put your credit union hat back on: What resources do you have in your operation that would help a campaign meet its goal? Credit unions are used to sorting and organizing data about potential recipients so they receive targeted messages, organizing mass mailings to large numbers of people, and handling dozens of incoming phone calls. So if a campaign manager needs to sort, stuff, and address hundreds of special mailings, couldn't your credit union help out? If a candidate wanted access to a small area with numerous desks and phones with direct-dialing capabilities, wouldn't your credit union's phone center, lobby, or other work area fit this need?

You have two options in making these company resources available to a campaign. First, you can rent the space, equipment, and other resources to campaign at cost. It will cost a campaign something to avail itself of your resources, but your costs in providing those services would be substantially below what the campaign would have to pay to use commercially available space.

Your second option would be to donate the space, equipment, or resources to a campaign for its use free of cost. Realize that allowing a campaign free use of your phone center to make fund-raising calls is a contribution of that equipment—telephones, desk space, line charges, and utilities—to the campaign. If you're a federal credit union, you are prohibited from making such a donation, but you could use the first option to provide those resources at cost. State credit unions can make such contributions to state candidates if their state's law allows corporate contributions. Credit unions cannot make direct contributions to federal candidates, so if it's a campaign for Congress, you are once again limited to the first option.

Another form of in-kind contribution that would be useful to a campaign is to host a reception or coffee to "Meet the Candidate" at your credit union. In addition to perhaps being able to contribute some attractive and convenient meeting space, this type of event allows the candidate to develop a positive association between your credit union and the community members that attend (assuming you have an open invitation to the public; look later in this chapter for ideas and rules about events that are limited solely to your credit union's members).

You could also make good use of your credit union's facilities by conducting a fund-raiser for the candidate at your credit union. Again, it makes the connection between your credit union and the candidate even tighter, and it also opens avenues for the candidate to another potential source of funds. It may sound like beating a drum, but money is crucial to successful campaigns, and candidates pay attention to people or groups they can count on for significant support.

Candidates pay attention to people or groups they can count on for significant support.

Chapter/Annual Meetings

Some credit union gatherings can still prove valuable for a candidate without necessarily including a money-raising component. Credit unions regularly put together meetings, such as chapter meetings or credit union annual meetings, that have dozens, and sometimes hundreds, of people in attendance. Is there a politician alive who wouldn't appreciate the opportunity to address a group like that? But there are certain factors to consider in putting such a meeting together.

First, structure the meeting to avoid unintended consequences of making the event into a campaign function. If you only include your chapter or members in the meeting, you don't have to worry about the in-kind contribution rules discussed previously. As a membership organization, your credit union or chapter is certainly allowed by election laws to communicate with its members about political issues (see the further discussion about partisan communications).

Second, make sure the candidate is comfortable with the topic you would like to have addressed. As a guest at your meeting, you should allow the candidate some latitude in selecting a topic with which he or she is comfortable and which fits the campaign theme. Hopefully, the candidate will be astute enough to include some thoughts about issues pertinent to credit unions (given the nature of the audience). But he or she shouldn't necessarily be expected to make that a focus of the speech.

Lastly, understand that these types of meetings are not lobbying visits. In other words, this is not the opportunity for a long, protracted discussion of some credit union issue that you feel is particularly pertinent. Meetings and speeches are "public" events (even though only your chapter or members are invited). And it isn't appropriate to embarrass a candidate by asking specific questions for which he or she has not had an opportunity to prepare, or to coerce a candidate into a position on some issue before studying it.

A candidate comes to your event to have an opportunity to deliver a message to a relatively large group of people at one time. Hopefully, he or she will remember the opportunity you've provided and add that event to the memory of the relationship you're establishing. Remember that these types of meetings are the candidate's opportunity, not yours, to speak out.

MEMBER EDUCATION/PARTISAN COMMUNICATIONS

The member-owner nature of credit unions provides us a unique opportunity in the world of politics. Federal election laws prohibit companies from sponsoring or engaging in communications about candidates or elections. However, these laws do allow organizations to communicate to their members about politics and related issues. Such direct communication between an organization and its members is called **partisan communications.** This provision allows credit unions to communicate freely with their members about candidates and issues because they are informing their members, not communicating with the general public.

Most credit unions have a ready-made vehicle for facilitating these communications: the newsletter. Practically every credit union sends a newsletter out to its members to inform them about current pertinent information. Usually, that information focuses on new product offerings, credit union rates and fees, or consumer advice. Given the relative importance that politics has assumed for credit unions, doesn't it make sense to devote at least some of your newsletter space to developments or information in that area? And if you're going to discuss politics and credit unions in your newsletter, think of the valuable service you can provide by highlighting candidates who have demonstrated or expressed their support for credit unions.

> *Most credit unions have a ready-made vehicle for facilitating communications: the newsletter.*

Remember, credit unions are uniquely positioned among financial institutions to take advantage of the membership nature of their clientele. So long as the form of communication is predominantly limited to the credit union's members, this partisan communication exception can be expanded beyond the credit union's newsletter to phone banks, special mailings, or membership meetings, such as the credit union's annual meeting.

The message we choose to communicate is up to us. It should be shaped by the credit union without influence by a particular candidate, so as to avoid the implication that the credit union is merely passing along that candidate's campaign message. Use these partisan communications to encourage members to donate to political causes, to vote, to contact legislators about credit union issues or positions, or simply to generate support for one or more candidates who have expressed their support for your credit union. Don't be afraid to let your members know how important the election process is to their credit union, and how they can support or encourage participation in many forms to guarantee that credit union issues remain at the forefront of candidates and legislators.

CHAPTER SIX

CREDIT UNIONS IN THE LEGISLATIVE PROCESS

In chapter 5, we outlined the various roles credit union people can take in the election process—basically directed toward building a relationship with candidates so that they come to appreciate credit unions and the important place they have in the local community. Now let's move forward and assume that your candidate was successful in the election—hopefully due in no small part to the enormous support received from credit unions.

Now the arena for the game of politics shifts from the election process to the legislative session. This chapter covers your activities in the context of the state legislature, since that's the arena with the most action and it allows for the greatest direct impact. But the tools and techniques apply equally well to federal issues in Congress, so adapt them accordingly.

The newly elected legislator has just spent months, perhaps even years, striving to become a player in the political game. He or she is entering a strange new world governed by arcane rules and procedures. To be successful, the legislator must learn to make backroom deals and establish covert alliances. The rules are established by a rigid power structure that can shift with the whims of just a few malcontents. All these dynamics are played out under the intense glare of public scrutiny, which shines on this process unlike any other arena in our culture. Even incumbents face different dynamics as new blood is injected into the legislative body, leadership challenges are launched, and the public evolves a new set of policy priorities that must be addressed.

In this chapter, we'll explore the different steps in the legislative process and the opportunities credit union people have to direct and influence legislation that affects them. Overall, the theme of your participation in the legislative process is a continuation of the goal we set in the election cycle: Build a relationship with the persons in power so that we are a respected voice relied on for input and guidance about credit union issues.

LEARNING THE RULES OF THE LEGISLATIVE GAME

No aspect of our culture is so hidebound to rules and tradition as the legislative process. Arcane pronouncements and procedures govern the process in such a way that it's not enough just to know what you want to accomplish; you must also know exactly how to get it done.

There's no question that the professional lobbyists with CUNA or your league should be the experts in the process. But even the most casual participant needs to know the basics of how an idea works its way through the legislature to become law (remember the process discussed in chapter 4) so that they know how and when they can exert their influence most effectively.

Your goal is to build on your relationship.

Your goal is to build on your relationship, established during the election process, and be viewed by your legislator as an important and capable ally. Most legislative bodies begin their work early in January following the election; make sure you're right there to enforce your candidate's good impression of you as a key player in this political arena and become a resource throughout the upcoming session. To help you fill this role in the legislative process, make sure you know the following information:

- *When does the legislative session start?* You need to know how soon to reconnect with your legislators once they're in office.
- *Who is in the leadership positions of Speaker of the House, President of the Senate, and majority and minority leaders in both houses?* You need to know who the ultimate gatekeepers are in the process—remember the role Newt Gingrich played in moving H.R. 1151 through the House of Representatives.
- *When are committees appointed and how are they structured?* You need to know who the key players are on matters that pertain to your credit union.
- *Who are the committee chairs and vice-chairs?* Again, the leadership role and gatekeeping function are crucial, even at the committee stage.

- *What's the process for introducing legislation, publishing bills, and moving them through the legislature?* You need to know how proposals are made, where to watch for potential threats, and the necessary steps to get an idea passed or killed.
- *What's the deadline for introducing bills and the process for amending bills previously introduced?* You need to know when you have a finite field of bills to track, which ones to focus on, and where the backdoor threats can come later on if you're successful in blocking negative legislation.
- *What's the final schedule for this legislative session?* Most state sessions end as of a certain date or after a certain number of legislative days, and bills introduced in one session usually aren't carried over, so you need to learn these procedures so you can figure out strategy and gauge the urgency in your messages.

The answers to these questions will give you a good working understanding of the legislative process so you'll recognize what your options are when it comes time to try to influence the outcome of legislation. That's what participation in the legislative game is all about—how to steer legislation, good or bad, to the outcome you desire. It's no small feat, but it's the ultimate goal of anyone in the political game. Review these questions in figure 6.1 to prepare for it.

Figure 6.1 Key Questions for Political Players

- When does the legislative session start?
- Who are the leaders—Speaker of the House, President of the Senate, and majority and minority leaders in both houses?
- When are committees appointed and how are they structured?
- Who are the committee chairs and vice-chairs?
- What's the process for introducing legislation, publishing bills, and moving them through the legislature?
- What's the deadline for introducing bills and what's the process for amending bills previously introduced?
- What's the final schedule for the legislative session?

Setting the Legislative Agenda

Knowing how the process works and getting involved in the political game won't do you much good unless you know what you want to accomplish. Entering the legislative arena without a clear agenda and sense of purpose is like going out onto a football field and trying to dribble a basketball before kicking it through the soccer goal. If you're going to be in the game, you better know what you want to do and how to do it successfully.

You better know what you want to do and how to do it successfully.

The crucial element for credit unions in getting our agenda accomplished is coordination. Standing alone, few if any credit unions have the money, power, or influence in the legislative process to command much attention. However, by coordinating efforts, we can bring to bear the combined power and influence of the credit union movement. Remember from chapter 2 this is why Filene and Bergengren formed state credit union leagues in the first place.

That coordination is a difficult balancing act, since not all credit unions have the same business plan or goals or fill the same niche in their communities. But that's why credit union political efforts should focus on our common threads—member ownership, cooperative principles, and not-for-profit status, among others—and make sure they remain unbroken.

As a trade association, your state league plays an essential role in bringing those divergent credit union voices into concert around a common agenda. Aside from all the other jobs your league may perform, its bedrock function is to act as the lens through which political efforts are focused—to create, preserve, and protect a favorable legislative environment for credit unions in that state. Since no credit union can be successful on its own, leagues must assume that role and shape the credit union agenda in each legislative session.

Most leagues have a **governmental affairs committee** made up of leading political figures from the credit unions in your state. If you're interested in helping to set the direction for your league's governmental affairs programs, contact your state league and offer to serve on the committee or one of its subcommittees. Just like in your credit union, enthusiastic and involved volunteers are always welcome, and the league should be no exception.

Relationship Management

So now you've gotten the word from your league about the purpose and direction credit unions are going to pursue during this legislative session. The next step is to communicate that agenda to your legislators. Short of becoming a legislator yourself, the only way you'll be able to influence the legislation necessary to successfully complete that agenda is to build that all-important relationship with those who do make the laws.

Hopefully, you've followed the process outlined in chapter 5 and gotten to know the candidate, impressed upon him or her the importance of credit unions and their issues, and had a role in the election. The next step is to inform that legislator about the credit union agenda for that session and communicate how accomplishing that agenda will help that legislator's constituents. Without a firm relationship established, your request will more than likely not be heard, because legislators usually have their own agendas. Remember that legislators want to help all the people who got them elected.

Properly managed, however, your relationship with your legislator will allow you the opportunity to lay out your agenda for the coming session. Remember to frame it in terms that will help that legislator's constituents or community. The legislator isn't there just to protect your credit union for its own sake; you need to put your credit union in the greater context of the community or district that the legislator was elected to represent.

Another benefit of developing a good working relationship with your legislator will be the opportunity to inform him or her on broader issues as well. A credit union doesn't exist in a vacuum; we're also affected by the same laws and follow most of the rules that impact small businesses of almost any type. Try to impress upon your legislator your ability and willingness to provide expertise and guidance on general business issues as well. The more the legislator comes to you for advice and information, the better you'll cement that relationship.

Try to impress upon your legislator your ability and willingness to provide expertise and guidance.

Use of Outside Legislative Counsel

If politics is a game, then one basic tenet holds as in every other game: No one plays it better than the professionals. There are professionals in the field of politics just as there are in any other form of human endeavor. Lobbyists are too often viewed negatively in our society, simply because all of politics is viewed as somewhat distasteful. There's certainly no group more closely tied in the public's mind to the negative aspects of politics than lobbyists. However, when you want to accomplish your legislative agenda, there's also no one more indispensable.

You need experts to guide you through any endeavor as complicated and convoluted as the legislative process. Most state leagues have one or more people on staff who direct their governmental affairs efforts. However, unless that person has been involved in the local political scene for a number of years, there's no way he or she can provide the same level of guidance and expertise as a competent professional lobbyist. Some state leagues have the resources to provide the expertise and continuity; more often, they rely on an outside lobbyist to supplement and guide their efforts.

In working with an outside lobbyist, focus on two fundamental principles. First, know what the lobbyist's role is in the process. Second, make sure the lobbyist has a clear understanding of your agenda. Let's explore these principles a little further.

Despite popular legend, few lobbyists have legislators "in their pockets," nor is a lobbyist's role to pay off legislators with lavish dinners, junkets to plush resorts, and illicit contributions. The best lobbyists engage in the relationship-building process that we've emphasized over the last several chapters—getting to know candidates, gauging their ability to succeed in their elections, providing assistance and guidance to those candidates who support the positions of that lobbyist's clients, and nurturing that relationship through the legislative process by providing advice and assistance to legislators. As professionals, however, it just stands to reason that lobbyists are more adept at accomplishing these processes than credit union amateurs.

The good news is that you can "purchase" this relationship and access by selecting the right lobbyist to help you with credit union issues. The right lobbyist can open doors of access to the halls of power in your legislature, wherever they may be. Knowing where they are is a key talent for a lobbyist as well. Their role is to give you professional insight into the legislative process, tell you how to get your agenda passed, and let you know where threats and problems arise so you can address them as early as possible.

Building relationships and credibility with legislators through lobbyists is a very effective entree. While it's no substitute for active, personal involvement in campaigns and the legislature, it supplements and strengthens the good work you've already done.

But let's make one thing clear: The duty to hire, manage, and direct a paid lobbyist should lie with your state league if it chooses to use one. Nothing would lead to dissension and dilution of your credit union agenda more quickly than several lobbyists each working independently on behalf of just a few credit union clients. Again, coordination and concentration of message is essential, so leave the managing of outside lobbying experts to the governmental affairs experts at your state league.

Coordination and concentration of message is essential.

The second important principle in using an outside lobbyist is to make sure he or she understands the credit union industry. You really cannot distill the credit union movement, its character, and its essence in a quick briefing with a committee chair two minutes before a hearing on an important bill. If the lobbyist is to provide access and understanding of the process, he or she must also have a broad understanding of the industry represented.

Your role is obviously not to quiz your league's lobbyist on the finer points of credit union philosophy. Leave the selection and education process to your league. But you can certainly offer your credit union's resources and assistance in that education process.

Take the time when you have the opportunity to offer background or support on credit union positions or proposals and what direct effect they'll have on your credit union's ability to provide services to your members. Involve the league's lobbyist in your credit union activities, including meetings of your credit union's governmental affairs committee (which you should set up—see chapter 7), your board or staff meetings, and even your annual meeting, to get a flavor of the unique nature and structure of credit unions.

LEGISLATIVE STAFF

No discussion of credit union involvement in the legislative process is complete without considering the legislative staff. By now, we're assuming that you have developed a close relationship with the legislators representing your home and credit union's districts. You may think that relationship entitles you to ready access to that legislator whenever you deem it necessary. That's not the case for even the closest of acquaintances.

Every legislator has a staff of professionals or volunteers. The size of the staff varies with the size and scope of the legislator's district, committee assignments and possible leadership positions, and ability to inspire willing volunteers to assist with the organization of that session's business. In a very real sense, the staff directs and controls the legislator more than you might expect. No one can organize and manage the complex number of demands placed on even the most reticent legislator without significant assistance. In building your relationship with a legislator, don't forget to include that legislator's staff in the process.

Normally, the people who were involved with the legislator's campaign may very well make up the bulk of the staff, because the legislator has obviously developed a good working relationship with those individuals. Many times, long-time legislative staff will also fill out the team because they have experience with prior sessions and can help a legislator get to know the process and how to best work within it.

Your interaction with a legislator's staff will usually take two forms. First, there's usually one person responsible for the legislator's schedule. That person books all appointments and meetings (it's too complicated if that responsibility is spread among a number of people). The **scheduler** is the primary gatekeeper for access to the legislator. Make sure you know the scheduler and that he or she understands your relationship with the legislator and knows that when you call for a meeting, you're not just another constituent but someone who is an important and trusted consultant. When you call, make sure the scheduler understands the level of urgency associated with your call or request. If you're setting up an appointment for next week when you'll be coming to town, don't demand a commitment that second. Wait until there is real urgency to your message and then try to impress that immediate urgency upon the scheduler.

The second person to get to know is the **staff specialist** responsible for your area of interest. Again, depending on the size of the staff, this person may be very specialized or have responsibility for a broad range of issues. This staffer usually conducts basic research in the areas assigned and is looked to when policy questions arise in that area.

Find out who on the legislator's staff is handling credit union or financial institution issues. Introduce yourself to that staffer and offer yourself as a resource for basic information. Become known as someone who can provide that staffer with background research and answers to specific policy questions that come up during the session. The more helpful you can be in making that staffer successful in his or her job, the more likely that person will be to listen to your point of view.

Bottom line, recognize that the legislator's staff holds an important supporting role in the political game. The legislator may be the superstar, but the staff plays a big part in that success. Treat staffers with respect and professional courtesy and try to develop a relationship. The legislator will look to the staff for the final word on many issues; make sure you've taken the opportunity to make your side known to that important person in the process.

Treat staffers with respect and professional courtesy and try to develop a relationship.

LOBBYING BASICS

Although it seems there are many players already participating in the political game at this point, you still have a chance to play an important role. There's plenty of work to do even in legislative sessions with the most unambitious agendas. Despite the number of professionals your league may have on staff or by contract working on behalf of credit unions, you need to take an active, participative role in lobbying during the legislative session.

Make sure you have a clear and comprehensive understanding of the credit union **legislative agenda** for that session. Many times in the past, credit unions simply were trying to skate through most legislative sessions undamaged. Our message to legislators for years had been, "Credit unions are healthy, members are happy, and we're doing a great job, so leave us alone." Anyone who's paid even the briefest attention to the current legislative climate for credit unions should know that those days are gone forever.

The bankers' campaign to reform the credit union movement into their image means that, at the very least, our agenda in every legislative session will be to fend off attacks against our tax exemption, field of membership policies, unique regulatory structure, and any other "differences" between us and banks. Add in the other challenges we might face, and it's easy to develop a very extensive defensive agenda. That doesn't even begin to address the affirmative steps you may choose to undertake in any given session, such as improvements in your state's credit union act.

The starting point for developing an agenda comes with an analysis of proposed legislation. Most state legislatures have thousands of bills introduced each session. Only a comparative handful are passed into law, but every one has to be weighed and evaluated for its potential impact on credit unions. While your league certainly has a system developed to accomplish that review, more eyes reviewing these proposals could certainly help. So an important role you can fulfill in the legislative process is to assist in that system. No matter what your position with the credit union, you have a unique perspective that may help in ferreting out potential problems, perceiving possible benefits, or just looking at a bill differently. Contact your league to find out about its bill review process and see if there is an active role you can assume.

Aside from the defensive agenda, more credit unions are pursuing affirmative proposals that improve their legal structure or framework. Two states, Oregon and Missouri, recently pursued field of membership legislation to forestall banker attacks. California fought a long and difficult battle to ease the impact of taxation on its state-chartered credit unions. Every state needs to periodically review and improve its credit union laws to make sure they reflect modern practices and afford each credit union appropriate powers to compete in the current financial marketplace. All these proposals begin at the league level. They were developed to address concerns raised by the league's credit unions and introduced to further their progress and development.

Many of these affirmative credit union proposals may be quite simple and direct, taking one word out here or adding a simple phrase there. Some bills, like the rewrites of credit union acts, are lengthy and complex proposals developed over months and with the input of numerous participants from many facets of the movement. Your involvement in drafting and refining these proposed bills will of course depend on your area of expertise and willingness to participate. Again, you won't know what opportunities are out there unless you become an active and involved participant in your league's governmental affairs program.

Your league's role in forming the agenda for the legislative session moves naturally into its responsibility to develop a strategy that gets that agenda accomplished. Hopefully, the league has a plan for either passing the legislation that has been developed or for identifying and blocking the bills that would be detrimental to credit unions. Your role in that plan can take many forms, but your participation is vital. Credit unions' main advantage in the legislative arena is "people power," so even if your only active role in the session is to show up whenever the league sends out the word, you're accomplishing an important role in the process.

Leagues organize a variety of events and meetings geared toward developing and enhancing a credit union presence throughout the legislative session. Following are some common activities you can participate in (and if your league doesn't organize one or more of these, encourage them to do so with your help and participation).

Your participation is vital.

Credit Union Day at the Capitol

Usually held very early in the session, this sort of event is designed as a show of force to legislators. The goal is to encourage as many credit union people as possible to show up for the activity. Make sure they are easily identifiable as credit union attendees by having prominent badges, pins, or other identification. Take the opportunity to reconnect with the legislators from your district. Let them know how many credit union people came by that day and make sure you reintroduce yourself to them, meet their staff (remember, they're the ultimate gatekeepers of access to the legislator), and familiarize yourself with the league's upcoming agenda that session. Begin to develop your role in that process and identify where and how you can lend a gentle nudge as necessary to move that agenda along.

Receptions During Session

In addition to an introductory day at the capitol, regularly scheduled receptions or meetings can also be effective in maintaining a consistent presence at the capitol. Leagues can organize periodic visits from credit unions representing different areas of the state to focus on particular legislators. Nothing makes a bigger impact than personal visits from constituents, particularly if they have had to travel some distance.

There isn't necessarily a specific agenda tied to these receptions, be they breakfast meetings, luncheons, or even cocktail or dinner parties. They should just be geared toward allowing credit union people to reinforce their commitment to the legislative process and show legislators that these people are an informed and active constituency. Of course, active participation in such receptions is everyone's job, once they're organized. Imagine what a terrible impression it makes when a legislator is expecting to meet with people from his or her district and hardly anyone bothers to make the trip. That legislator isn't likely to be interested in your issues in the future if you don't pay attention and remain active throughout the process.

Rallies

There's no better demonstration of credit union people power than a loud, vocal celebration in support of the credit union position. During the 1997 legislative session, the Pennsylvania League was supporting a bill that would ban surcharges on automated teller machines. The league's rally in support of its bill attracted over nine hundred attendees and brought sharp media focus, both locally and through the credit union trade press, onto their agenda. That same session, the Oregon League organized the largest rally of any group during that session in support of its field of membership bill, with over twelve hundred attendees. It was covered by every major newspaper and television station in the state.

> *These rallies demonstrate the breadth and depth of concern about issues.*

These rallies demonstrate the breadth and depth of concern about issues. They force legislators to take notice and develop positions on issues that may be stuck in the process or otherwise ignored. Legislators don't relish the idea of making difficult policy decisions, such as whether to support banks or credit unions on particular legislation. Rallies bring a large group of people, not to mention public and media attention, to a particular issue.

Any rally should have the following elements to be successful:

- **Numbers.** What if you threw a rally and no one came? The chief element in generating any kind of legislator or media attention is to have large numbers of people attend. You need to think creatively about how to generate large numbers of rally participants from your credit union. The factors to review of course depend on the logistics of how far you have to travel and time of the rally, for example. But consider such ideas as closing the credit union in the middle of the day so staff can attend the rally. Closing the credit union gives you an opportunity to communicate to your members about the rally and encourage their participation. Let members know that the closure resembles what it would be like if the credit union were closed forever, an interesting contrast if the rally is about field of membership or something equally important to the credit union's survival.

    If you have to travel some distance to a rally, join with other credit unions and hire a bus or other form of group transportation. Use the travel time to brief people about the issues and the scheduled events of the day. Invite local media to share transportation with you—if you have a two- or three-hour trip to the rally, you'll never get a better time to brief a reporter about your issues, provide a deeper understanding of credit unions, and tell the background for the story.

    If your credit union is close to the capitol, hire buses for members to attend. Organize pick-up/drop-off sites around the area and advertise them (through your newsletter or special mailing) to members ahead of time. Since members are local and the rally will probably only take a few minutes (most shouldn't be scheduled for longer than thirty to thirty-five minutes), you have the best chance of generating real numbers in support of the event. Make it as easy as possible for members to attend to encourage participation.

- **Message.** The rally needs to have a focused message, a narrow target audience, and a specific idea to communicate. A rally in support of credit unions in general will lack direction and purpose—it should have direct relevance to a particular issue at that point to be effective. Your legislative agenda for that session is probably clear-cut, and the rally should be targeted to help support that agenda.

    Realize that rallies take weeks, if not months, of planning and preparation to be successful. You may not know what your specific message in support of your overall agenda will be for that rally until the week or days immediately before. That doesn't mean you shouldn't organize a rally; it just means that everyone must remain flexible so the specific message (push the committee for action on your bill, support a floor vote in the House or Senate, celebrate a successful passage by either chamber, urge the other chamber to move quickly, for example) can be developed right at the last minute for greatest effect.

- **Media.** A rally of hundreds or thousands of credit union supporters doesn't mean much unless someone hears about it. Involve the media in the rally through as many avenues as possible. You probably have the best contacts with your local media through your credit union's marketing personnel. Or just the credit union's presence in the local community may be an advantage that the league cannot match. Use those contacts to inform the media of the upcoming event. Provide them background on your credit union and the particular issue that's the subject of the rally. Involve them in the preparation and participation so they can add a local flavor to their coverage. And follow up after the rally to thank them for their coverage and to answer any remaining questions.

    When organizing a rally, don't forget to "feed" the media what they will need to improve their coverage. Prepare press kits with information about the rally issue and background materials. Get the kits out to reporters well in advance of the rally to let them review the material and clear up any questions. Don't forget to include elements in your rally that make for good media coverage, such as colorful posters or balloons, quality sound systems for projection and recording purposes, and adequate access for cameras or media trucks.

    Remember to arrange for spokespersons from the credit unions who are available to reporters for comments or anecdotes about the issues. Make sure you use articulate, informed people for this role. If you prepare your spokespersons and steer the reporters to them, you'll project your message much more effectively through whatever coverage you do receive. Match up reporters for out-of-town media with credit union spokespersons from that area. Stories always have a better impact if there's a local flavor to the coverage.

    That brings up a point about local media outlets. Certainly everyone wants the immediacy of television or radio coverage, but don't underestimate the value of newspapers. You probably would focus on the big daily newspaper that includes your area, but don't forget the small, local newspapers in your community, even if they're just a weekly publication. The other hidden benefit of this local media coverage is that most legislators monitor these small papers in their districts for insight into the hot local issues. You probably stand a better chance of coverage as well, since you're not competing with the major metropolitan media outlets. That's why giving these events a local flavor is so critical to broad exposure.

- **Legislators.** Remember who your ultimate audience is—the legislators who are currently considering the issue that is the subject of the rally. Focus on ways to demonstrate your presence on rally day, such as delivering postcards, petitions, or balloons to the legislator's offices. (That's another great activity for passengers during that long bus ride to the rally, should you have one—filling out postcards to be delivered that day to their legislator). Organize the rally's time and place so it gets the legislator's attention. Oregon held its rally on the capitol's front steps at noon so everyone leaving for lunch couldn't help but notice the throngs of people outside.

  Whatever form your communication with legislators takes through the process of this rally, make sure the message you deliver is focused and direct. Be specific about the issue at hand and about the action or outcome you are seeking to achieve ("Vote yes on the credit union field of membership bill"; "Vote no on the bankers 'Tax Credit Unions' legislation"; "Limit Bank ATM Surcharges"). Simple, direct, targeted, and clear messages are the most effective.

Grassroots Lobbying Activities

As you remember from chapter 4, every bill has to be passed out of committee before it can be acted on by the full House or Senate. Committees usually hold one or more hearings on a bill before passing it out, although sometimes if the issue is being considered during the final days of a legislative session, the time frame can be compressed considerably and bills can be moved out by floor action without committee consideration. That's why timely and effective communication from your league on the bill's status is so crucial.

Prior to the hearing, the league must communicate with legislators on that committee about the bill and its impact on credit unions. Oftentimes, that effort requires a number of letters, phone calls, or other messages in support of the credit union position. Your part is to work within the timing and schedule laid out by the league, so those messages reach the legislators at the most appropriate and effective time. Coordination is crucial, for a barrage of letters weeks before any action is scheduled are forgotten by the time the hearing or vote occurs, and a message delivered after the action is taken won't help to correct an unfortunate outcome.

When the time comes for you to communicate with your legislator, you'll once again need to take the cue from your league as to the amount of time you have to deliver your message and the best method to communicate. Generally, however, personal letters or notes handwritten by constituents are the most effective form of delivering a message. The person writing took the time to write, and they often tell a personal story or reflect an individual perspective on the issue. This commitment of time and personal feelings demonstrates the importance of the issue to that person. Messages delivered by e-mail can be said to have the same attributes and are another good form of communicating. However, the medium is too new to judge whether it's viewed with the same impact as a personal, handwritten note. Many legislative offices simply aren't equipped to respond effectively to e-mail or log those messages into their systems.

Personal letters or notes handwritten by constituents are the most effective form of delivering a message.

Phone calls and faxes offer an immediacy to the message that isn't available with a handwritten letter or note. The difficulty with these forms of communication is that the message is not as clear or permanent. But, obviously, if the issue is moving quickly through the system, you may need to use a method that allows for faster delivery. The other advantage of phone calls and faxes is it is easier to generate raw numbers of responses or messages on an issue. Credit union members will often call or fax a brief message (especially if your credit union makes it easy by having a phone or fax available in your lobby for members to use) whereas they may not take the time to write a personal note. But don't let the ease of use lure people to these methods unless the time element makes them necessary—always encourage personal, handwritten communication when the circumstances allow.

The least effective form of communication with legislators is preprinted postcards that flood their offices or petitions that reflect a raw (albeit hopefully large) number of signatures. These methods do have their place and if they are the best your members will do, don't turn them away. But coordinated mass-mailings are too easy to orchestrate and don't reflect the depth or impact that a personal expression on the issue would. If all the credit union member will do is take two seconds to do something, then make a postcard or petition available to them. But try to encourage them to take a little more time to communicate how important the issue is by putting it in individual terms.

Fortunately, credit unions have a number of advantages when it comes to generating these numerous responses. Use your credit union's resources to target particular groups of members and match them up with the appropriate legislator. Most credit unions can do a ZIP code sort on their data processing systems to find out which members live in which zones. Match those up with the ZIP codes that correspond to a legislator's district (contact your state election office or the league for this information) and solicit those members to write their particular legislator. Let the legislator know how many individual voters you have in the district by going through this ZIP code sorting process. CUNA has developed Project Zip Code to do this; all it takes are disks of your credit union's members with their addresses for sorting. Participate in CUNA's program if you haven't already.

Leagues and CUNA are also using increasingly sophisticated methods to reach their member credit unions. You can adapt these as available to reach your membership. Blast faxes to credit unions, as well as phone trees to deliver messages quickly, are being developed to speed up communication and allow leagues to help credit unions tailor their messages to their legislators to fit circumstances. Talk to your league about using the most effective and efficient form of communication to get the message out in a timely basis to the people who need to act on it.

Hearing and Voting Days

As mentioned, any bill making its way through the legislative process to passage will have at least two hearings and two full votes, one in each chamber. Usually, those days require another show of support for the credit union position. Get to know the route to your state capitol. When the session is on, plan on making a number of trips in support of the credit union agenda.

Again, you have a simple job once you hear about a hearing or vote on a credit union bill where the league wants a show of force—show up. It may seem like a little matter, but it really is important. If one of the legislators with whom you've developed a relationship is on the committee hearing the bill, or in the chamber considering it for a full vote, your attendance is crucial. You need to demonstrate to that legislator the importance of the bill under consideration by taking the time to show up. Make that legislator take a position on your bill with you in attendance and with full knowledge that you will hold him or her accountable for the action they take.

The Missouri League faced a crucial vote in the House on its field of membership bill and it failed the first time through—not because so many people voted against the bill, but because not enough legislators showed up to vote in favor of it. Most legislative bodies require a bill to receive a majority vote to pass it out even if not all the members are present to vote. Luckily, the Missouri League was able to have the bill brought up days later for reconsideration and it passed overwhelmingly. But this experience demonstrates the need for individual vigilance in making sure legislators know that your bill is up for a vote and you're watching them. If you do travel to the state capitol for a hearing or a vote, make sure you stop by the legislator's office, drop off your business card, and say hello to the staff. Again, reinforce your image as an active and involved participant in the legislative process.

Reinforce your image as an active and involved participant in the legislative process.

Once the vote is taken, whether it's in committee or the full House or Senate, follow up with your legislator accordingly. Thank him or her for a favorable vote and express your appreciation for the support. If the legislator voted against credit unions, you still need to maintain that relationship. Find out what the problem was and address the concerns raised by the legislator. Remember, there's very little you can do to change who is in office, so try to rebuild your relationship and turn the legislator into a credit union supporter. If for some reason the relationship is irretrievable, go back to chapter 5 concerning involvement in the election process and start all over again in the next election.

CHAPTER SEVEN

CREATING A POLITICAL CULTURE IN YOUR CREDIT UNION

By now, you realize how important governmental affairs and political action are to your credit union and its future. We've tried to give you suggestions for becoming more effective at the political game; a game in which every credit union must play its part. But if the credit union movement is to maximize its role and become a major player in that game, it takes more than an individual commitment from you. It's going to take a commitment by your entire credit union: its volunteers, its staff, and its members. We've discussed the different roles for each, but let's wrap up with a broader discussion about incorporating governmental affairs into your credit union's culture.

MISSION STATEMENT OR VISION

Almost every credit union engages in the planning process to establish goals and direction for the future. The first product of that planning process is a **mission statement** or **vision** that defines the credit union's purpose. Most mission statements talk about serving members' financial needs, adhering to cooperative principles, recognizing volunteer boards, and so on.

Have you incorporated governmental affairs during your credit union's planning process? Given the importance of governmental affairs and their influence on your credit union's future, you should consider including this component in your credit union's mission. After all, the laws and rules credit unions fall under define what they can be and do, so in a very real sense, they've already determined your mission to some degree.

The next step in the planning process after establishing a mission or vision is to develop **key result areas.** These are areas where your board and staff should direct special efforts during the upcoming planning period—the next year, or two, or five—however long you plan out for your credit union. Governmental affairs should be near the top of the list of key result areas.

From that prioritization, your next step is to develop **plans** and **goals** that fulfill your responsibility in each key area. Set measurable guidelines when incorporating governmental affairs into the planning process by discussing specific tasks or strategies, creating deadlines for completion or regular updates for ongoing practices, and assigning specific responsibility to individual staff, board, or committee members for implementation. Start small if you must, but make sure you start.

Since these planning goals typically set the performance standards for management, staff, or volunteers, incorporating governmental affairs into the process will result in that area being a priority for everyone. That's the first step in making governmental affairs part of your credit union's culture.

BOARD RESPONSIBILITY AND COMMITMENT

The board of directors has a great deal of autonomy to set direction for the credit union. The board answers directly to the members, who formally check in only once a year at the annual meeting. If the board chooses to make governmental affairs participation a priority, members would hardly be expected to object—especially, again, in light of important events these days. On the other hand, practically any member is eligible to run for the director's position, so leadership and education on governmental affairs is particularly important as part of board development and succession.

Another way to demonstrate the board's commitment to governmental affairs is to establish a governmental affairs committee in the board structure. Making such a committee a permanent part of your credit union's leadership demonstrates the importance of that area to members and staff. The committee can either be composed solely of board members or can be expanded to include other volunteers, management, or staff representatives who want to direct the form and structure of the credit union's governmental affairs activities.

To demonstrate the board's commitment establish a governmental affairs committee in the board structure.

That's the most logical role for that committee—to take responsibility for directing the various activities the credit union undertakes in the way of political action. If your credit union is going to host fund-raisers and receptions, report on candidates from its district, include newsletter profiles and inserts about politicians and current issues, participate in league events like capitol briefings, and travel to hearings and voting sessions, then someone in your credit union should coordinate it all. Coordination needs to involve more than just one person. The committee structure allows for development of your credit union's activities in these areas, ready communication channels to all levels of volunteers and staff (especially if each has a role on the committee), and easier distribution of duties and responsibilities when these events or activities occur.

Even if you feel your credit union lacks the resources to rise to the level of commitment to governmental affairs that we've suggested, at the very least your board should recognize the importance of including governmental affairs as a priority in credit union operations at some level. Consequently, the board needs to provide staff and management the latitude to participate to the highest possible level, whatever that might be. Boards at least need to recognize that staff will spend some time fulfilling responsibilities in this area and should be allowed the time and resources to keep up the credit union's end in the political game.

STAFF AND PROFESSIONALS' COMMITMENT

Credit union staff members should have a particular interest in credit union political action. If the bankers' attacks or our own inattention to governmental affairs eliminates credit unions as we know them, board and committee volunteers will lose an important institution and the ability to continue serving members through our financial cooperatives. For the staff and professionals, their very careers and chosen livelihood are at stake. Wouldn't you think that reality would provide sufficient motivation for staff and professionals to become involved in political action?

Of course, there are issues other than motivation. For staff and professionals to make a commitment to governmental affairs activities, management and the board must allocate the time and resources necessary to perform those activities. There are a number of ways for that commitment to be communicated from management and the board to the staff and professionals.

Leading the Way

Management and board members must take an active leadership role by participating in political action activities organized by the credit union. They should be the first persons to volunteer to attend scheduled events, write the PAC checks for donations to state and federal funds, and present a visible commitment to this area of activities.

Investing Time

Staff and professionals also need to be given the time to participate in various governmental affairs activities, including the time necessary to plan and prepare for activities. Committee meetings should be held during work hours, or at least make it clear that those meetings are job-related and compensate nonexempt employees for their time. Allow employees the time to attend evening receptions or fund-raisers for candidates in the credit union's district, again at the company's expense. After all, their participation in these political activities are investments in the credit union's future legislative health, and investments always carry some level of cost. Compensating the time and effort of your credit union's staff and professionals is a prudent investment.

Spreading the Word

In addition to time, make sure your staff and professionals are specifically invited and encouraged to participate in your credit union's governmental affairs activities. Many times, the invitation to a campaign event from a candidate or call to action from the league sits fallow on the credit union manager's desk or gets lost in the credit union's distribution channels. Your credit union's management and board should make a special point of highlighting upcoming political events and making sure staff and professionals are encouraged to attend. Staff and professionals have a stake in the credit union's future as well and should be able to fully participate in its preservation and success. Streamline your communication channels so staff, professionals, and even volunteers who have expressed an interest in governmental affairs activities learn about them quickly and feel free to participate.

Oftentimes, these events arise quickly as last-minute arrangements fall into place or a slot at an event opens up. Election campaigns at all levels are neither the most organized nor coordinated organizations. Recall some of the events described in the Georgia League's work with Speaker Newt Gingrich's campaign. Treat these opportunities as rewards (people interested in politics should be enthusiastic about participating) and make sure they are handed to those individuals who have demonstrated their interest in and commitment to the political process.

Investing Money

Ensure that your credit union's governmental affairs activities are adequately budgeted and paid for. Incidental costs to your participation are bound to arise. Plan for added mailing costs when putting out a flyer to members about a candidate. Budget some overtime for nonexempt staff if they need extra time to complete their regular work because of a political commitment. Consider direct contributions for state-chartered credit unions where that option is available.

Knowing What to Avoid

One element of the political game you definitely want to avoid is playing around with phony campaign contributions. Make sure that your budgeting and expense process for governmental affairs does not include bogus expense reimbursements to individuals to "make up" for their direct political contributions. If your credit union is barred by law from making political contributions, either because it is a federal credit union or because of state or federal election laws, understand that money "passed through" a person's individual funds is not a lawful alternative. For example, eight people from your credit union sign up for a $50-a-plate political fund-raiser for the U.S. representative from your credit union's district. Those people all write individual checks for $50 to cover the cost of the dinner. (Remember only individuals and PACs are allowed to make federal campaign contributions.) It will appear at least a little suspicious if, that same week, those same eight people coincidentally claim $50 each of miscellaneous expenses to be reimbursed by the credit union.

Even if your practices are not as blatant as that, reimbursing employees or volunteers for false expenses to subsidize their participation in political action is just as much a violation of the election laws as your credit union paying the money directly to the campaign. The credit union's staff, management, and volunteers must be willing to make a personal commitment to the political process, and that includes committing their personal funds, especially when that is the only avenue available to fund federal and some state campaigns.

If you try hard enough, you can dream up any number of ways to get around these restrictions on corporate contributions. Every election year, the newspapers are full of groups and individuals who have been caught in similar indiscretions. Yes, other companies probably do pass through contributions to candidates. The point is that with our burgeoning political power and relative innocence in the game of government, the last thing the credit union movement needs is an election scandal.

Keep your credit union's financial participation in politics above reproach at all times. If you want to make sure that paid staff members are adequately compensated so they can afford to participate in the political process, there's no sin in that, so long as employees recognize those funds as compensation and have the freedom to use them as they wish. The money paid to employees is compensation, and how they spend it cannot be controlled or directed by supervisors, management, or the credit union board. Let's hope that employees' sense and responsibility lead them all to do their part in furthering credit union political action.

> *Keep your credit union's financial participation in politics above reproach at all times.*

Adding to Job Descriptions

Perhaps the most concrete way for management and boards to convey the importance of political action and governmental affairs is to specifically incorporate responsibility for these areas into staff job descriptions. The management team at your credit union should definitely have governmental affairs as some component of its responsibility. Putting that specific duty in a job description not only emphasizes the importance of participation in that process, it also allows the individual the direction and freedom to fulfill those responsibilities as part of the job, not just as some "outside" activity.

The direction to participate in governmental affairs can take many forms, but it definitely should be included. In some cases, the job description can be specifically tailored to the individual's anticipated role, such as making a person chair of the credit union's governmental affairs committee or assigning the duty of coordinating the credit union's activities in that area. Alternatively, the description could say that some outside political activity is expected. Many management descriptions include similar outside activities, such as participation in civic groups or charitable work. Make political action activities, like volunteering on a campaign, working with league events, or attending meetings or forums with legislators, a specific job requirement.

The job descriptions for all staff members can include some component of governmental affairs activities. Encourage participation in political events organized or hosted by the credit union, such as receptions or fund-raisers. Give staff credit for political action activities as part of continuing education or community involvement requirements, if you have them for your staff.

> *Encourage participation in political events organized or hosted by the credit union.*

Informing and Motivating

In addition to incorporating governmental affairs into staff job descriptions, make a point of including governmental affairs updates in regular staff activities. Staff meetings should contain an update on the political issues of the day and announcements about upcoming events. Governmental affairs committee meeting minutes should be disseminated to or discussed with everyone in the credit union. Participation on the committee should be open to people at all levels of the organization.

Keep the topic foremost in all your activities, and staff will soon see the importance political action has in your credit union and become involved. Even if you can't define a role for staff members at this time, move the issue of governmental affairs to near the top of your credit union's agenda, and staff will find a way to participate and support your credit union's efforts in this area. When they come to you with suggestions, keep an open mind and remember the goal of having everyone behind the credit union's efforts in the political arena.

INTEGRATING POLITICAL ACTION INTO YOUR CORPORATE CULTURE

We've given you suggestions for involving your credit union's volunteers, management, and staff in the area of governmental affairs. The simple truth is that no one in your credit union will treat governmental affairs as a priority until it becomes integrated in your corporate culture and a recognized priority. The idea of playing in the political game is foreign to most of us. Many credit unions just want to be left alone to serve members and provide the best financial services possible. But credit unions have assumed far too great a role in the lives of members to ever crawl back behind the shield of a protectionist ideology. Like it or not, the credit union movement is fully immersed in the political game and, as with any game, those who don't play it well will be the losers. Members, volunteers, and staff have too much at stake to let the fabric and nature of credit unions be shaped by others. Only by involving each and every credit union in our cooperative struggle to gain recognition and authority in the political process can we succeed.

To demonstrate that commitment, integrate governmental affairs into the culture of your credit union.

Your credit union's participation in this game is vital. Our political strength flows from the millions of credit union members in this country who are passionate about preserving that choice for their financial services. If your members lack passion for your credit union and its role in governmental affairs, it's because you still need to make that case more clearly. The best way to demonstrate that commitment is by integrating governmental affairs into the culture of your credit union.

Every facet of your credit union's operations should somehow relate back to its proper role in politics and government. If you don't think every area in your credit union relates to politics in some way, just review the long list of laws and regulations that govern, control, or influence every part of your operation, and you'll soon see the connection. Since those laws and rules are integrated in your credit union's corporate structure and operation, don't you think the ability to define and shape those laws and rules should be similarly emphasized?

Here's a plan of action for incorporating governmental affairs into your credit union's corporate culture and making political action a part of your credit union's everyday life:

1. Develop goals in the areas of political action and governmental affairs during your credit union's next planning process. Decide where you need to prioritize your efforts based on your current level of participation, available time and resources to devote to this area (perhaps by borrowing from areas you now recognize as less crucial to your credit union's survival), and activities that will maximize your credit union's relationship with its elected state and federal representatives.

2. Establish a governmental affairs committee in your credit union. Encourage participation from volunteers, management, and staff. You might even develop separate committees for each. Provide them the authority to develop and coordinate your credit union's political activities. Make sure their activities are adequately budgeted and carry out the goals you've established in the planning process.

3. Make governmental affairs a visible part of your credit union's culture. Establish a place in the lobby with the latest updates on governmental affairs and political activities. Include an opportunity for members to register to vote so they see the connection between active participation in the political process and your credit union's success. When you participate in political activities, make sure people know you're there on behalf of your credit union by wearing stickers, badges, shirts, hats, or whatever memorabilia you've developed that let people know who you're there to support.

4. Reward and recognize staff members for their commitment to adopting political action as their cause. Let them find their own way to participate in these activities and encourage them accordingly when they show initiative. At the very least, encourage everyone to vote by holding a raffle on election day with the ballot stubs. Find a way to make politics and the credit union's future important to them and show them their role in making it a success.

5. Lastly, make personal commitments to actively participate in the activities organized or sponsored by the governmental affairs committee. Provide the support, encouragement, and participation they need to make their plans successful. After all, our most valuable player in the political game is you, and all the other people just like you who are part of the credit union

movement in this country. We will fail without your support. But with the active participation of every one of the thousands of credit union volunteers, management professionals, and staff, plus the combined power of over seventy-seven million credit union members, we will shape our political future and continue to provide cooperative financial services.

APPENDIX

NCUA Documents

NCUA General Counsel Opinion Letter 92-0613, June 17, 1992

June 17, 1992

Mitchell B. Klein
General Counsel
Police and Fire
Federal Credit Union
901 Arch Street
Philadelphia, PA 19107-2495

Re: Permissible Political Activities (Your Letter of May 26, 1992)

Dear Mr. Klein:

You requested an opinion regarding the extent to which a Federal credit union ("FCU") may engage in political activity. The Federal Election Campaign Act prohibits an FCU from making "a contribution or expenditure in connection with any election to any political office, or in connection with any primary election or political convention or caucus held to select candidates for political office. . . ." 2 U.S.C. ~441b; see also 11 C.F.R. ~114.2 NCUA Interpretive Ruling and Policy Statement ("IRPS") No. 79-6, Donations/Contributions, does not apply to political contributions. IRPS 79-6, 44 Fed. Reg. 56691 (October 2, 1979). NCUA has opined that in order to be a valid exercise of an FCU's incidental authority that any political contributions must be legal under applicable federal and state law, not so excessive as to be a waste of corporate assets or a breach of safety and soundness, and that the FCU must receive something of monetary value (as opposed to goodwill) in return. An FCU may endorse a candidate if permissible under applicable federal and state law.

FCUs may be able to make contributions to certain political action committees, such as those organized by state associations. See 11 C.F.R. ~114.8. However, it should also be noted that FCUs are prohibited from making either a loan or investment to a trade association, nor are political contributions a preapproved credit union service organization activity. 12 U.S.C. ~~1757(5)(D) and 1757(7)(I); see also 12 C.F.R. ~701.27(b)(l(iii), (d)(5)(i)–(ii). NCUA does not have jurisdiction over Federal Election Campaign Act issues, and for further information we suggest you contact: Office of General Counsel, Federal Election Commission, 999 E Street, NW, Washington, DC 20463 (telephone 202/219–3690). We also suggest that you research state law for information regarding state restrictions. See, e.g. Pa. Stat. Ann., tit. 25, ~3253 (Purdon, 1991 Supp.) ("It is unlawful . . . for any corporation . . . to make a contribution or expenditure in connection with the election of any candidate or for any political purpose whatever. . . .") For further information, you may wish to contact either the Commonwealth of Pennsylvania or the Pennsylvania Credit Union League.

Sincerely,

Hattie M. Ulan
Associate General Counsel

GC/MEC:sg
SSIC 3800
92–0613

NCUA GENERAL COUNSEL OPINION LETTER 92-1202, MARCH 3, 1993

March 3, 1993

John J. McKechnie, III
Director, Political Action
Credit Union Legislative Action Council
of Credit Union National Association, Inc.
805 15th Street, NW
Suite 300
Washington, DC 20005–2207

Re: Political Action Committee ("PAC") Fund-raising Program

Dear Mr. McKechnie:

You requested that NCUA permit federal credit unions ("FCUs") to collect funds from its members on behalf of a political action committee ("PAC") and in exchange provide the member with an item of nominal value, such as a candy bar. Under the representations made by you in your letter of November 20, 1992, and under the limitations discussed in this letter, NCUA would consider such a program a valid exercise of incidental authority by an FCU. NCUA strongly recommends that FCUs contact either the Federal Election Commission or their own legal counsel before engaging in this program to ensure compliance with applicable election laws.

PROGRAM PROPOSAL

You represent to NCUA the following features of your proposed program. Under your program proposal, state credit union leagues or their PACs or a national trade association's PAC would buy the candy bars (or other items of nominal value), and the candy bars would be provided at no cost to FCUs that had given prior permission to be solicited, as required by Federal Election Commission ("FEC") regulations. The FCU would be provided with a free standing candy dispenser with a collection box for any donations made. Only FCU members who contribute to the league PAC, or directly to the Credit Union Legislative Action Council ("CULAC"), a national trade association's PAC, could receive candy bars, however, the FCU would not be under any duty to ensure this. The FCU would collect the contributions and forward all proceeds to the appropriate PAC. The FCU would not charge for this service, and all proceeds would be forwarded periodically to the appropriate PAC. The FCU would not purchase the candy bars, nor make any solicitations for the PAC from FCU members.

ANALYSIS

FCUs have authority "to exercise such incidental powers as shall be necessary or requisite to enable it to carry on effectively the business for which it is incorporated." 12 U.S.C. ~1757(17). In Arnold Tours, Inc. v. Camp, 472 F.2d 427 (1st Cir. 1972), a court defined incidental powers for national banks as:

> [an activity] that is convenient or useful in connection with the performance of one of the bank's established activities under the National Bank Act. If this connection between an incidental activity and an express power does not exist, the activity is not authorized as an incidental power. 472 F.2d 427, 432.

In American Bankers Association v. Connell, 447 F.Supp. 296 (D.D.C. 1978), the court applied the "convenient or useful" test of incidental powers to FCUs. Therefore, in order for an activity to be incidental it must be convenient or useful in performing an express power of an FCU. In this regard, you state the following:

> A[n FCU's] participation in this program would be a permissible exercise of powers incidental to all of the fundamental, explicit powers under Section 1757 of the [FCU] Act—such as the authority to make loans to members and accept members' share deposits. Credit unions' involvement in political activities—such as support of the state league PACs or CULAC through the candy bar program—is essential to the preservation of credit unions as unique financial institutions.

Banks and others that view themselves as competitors of [FCUs] routinely lobby Congress to change the nature of credit unions and restrict their ability to serve the borrowing and saving needs of their members. In addition to counterbalancing anti-credit union lobbies, credit unions must also be politically active since Congress regularly considers consumer protection measures that impact on credit union operations. It is imperative that a political climate exists on Capitol Hill that does not jeopardize the future of credit unions and their ability to exercise express powers under the FCU Act. One of the most effective ways to achieve such an atmosphere in Congress is to help elect, through campaign contributions and grassroots involvement, candidates who understand the importance of credit unions in the financial marketplace. Collecting contributions for CULAC or a state league PAC from members through programs that are legal under the FEC Act, such as the candy bar program, is unquestionably useful for a[n FCU] (under the ABA v. Connell standard) and is an activity that clearly is an incidental power.

To reinforce our argument that political action is a fundamental, if not explicit, power for [FCUs], we note that it is a permissible exercise of incidental powers for a[n FCU] to belong to a trade association, whose key role is to help ensure the passage of favorable legislation and defeat detrimental proposals. Organizing and maintaining a PAC to pool resources of individuals to elect candidates who support credit unions are necessary and legitimate functions of a trade association. If a credit union is able to pay dues to a trade association which supports candidates through a PAC, it should be able to participate in specific fund-raising programs permitted under the FEC Act, including the candy bar program outlined in this letter. Letter, pp. 2–3.

NCUA finds your appeal persuasive and well-reasoned. However, NCUA has no authority to interpret or enforce election laws. Therefore, since NCUA has a responsibility to ensure that no FCUs violate any applicable laws, NCUA urges FCUs to consult with their own legal counsel regarding participation in this program before engaging in it. Furthermore, as stated in the preamble to the analogous NCUA

Interpretive Ruling and Policy Statement No. 79-6 ("IRPS No. 79-6"): (1) Article VIII, Section 8 of the [FCU] Bylaws, requires that the minutes of the board of directors' meeting at which participation in such a program is authorized shall reflect the extent and nature of such participation; and (2) Article XIX, Section 4, of the [FCU] Bylaws, concerning conflicts of interest by officials and employees of an FCU, is applicable to the activities covered in this opinion. (FCU officials involved with any credit union PAC should recuse themselves from consideration of their FCU's participation in this program once presented to the FCU's board. We do not believe that an FCU official whose only involvement with a PAC is a financial contribution would normally necessitate recusal. However, serving on a PAC in any official capacity would necessitate recusal.) See IRPS No. 79-6, 44 Fed. Reg. 56691 (October 2, 1979) (enclosed). Under these conditions, and in accord with the representations made by CULAC as stated in this opinion, FCUs may engage in your proposed program as a legitimate exercise of incidental authority.

Sincerely,

Hattie M. Ulan
Associate General Counsel
GC/MEC:sg
SSIC 3210
92-1202

NCUA INTERPRETIVE RULING AND POLICY STATEMENT (IRPS) 79-6, JULY 10, 1979

July 10, 1979

IRPS No. 79-6—Donations/Contributions

AGENCY: National Credit Union Administration

ACTION: Interpretation of General Applicability

SUMMARY: This statement sets forth the National Credit Union Administration's interpretation of the incidental power a Federal credit union possesses to make donations. The Administration interprets the incidental powers clause of the Federal Credit Union Act (§ 107(15)) to permit a Federal credit union to make reasonable donations to tax exempt organizations under Section 501(c)(3) of the Internal

Revenue Code. This interpretation should result in an increase in community funds that are used for diverse charitable and educational needs of the public.

EFFECTIVE DATE: This statement will become effective immediately upon publication.

ADDRESS: National Credit Union Administration, 2025 M Street, N.W., Washington, D.C., 20456

FOR FURTHER INFORMATION CONTACT: Edward J. Dobranski, Senior Attorney, Office of General Counsel, National Credit Union Administration, at the above address. Phone (292) 632–4870.

SUPPLEMENTARY INFORMATION: The Administration is frequently asked whether Federal credit unions (FCU's) may make contributions or donate funds to various organizations. In the past, the Administration held that an FCU may donate its funds only if the FCU would derive a direct benefit from such donation or contribution.

The Administration, in accord with an increasing number of jurisdictions, realizes that a cooperative (e.g., a FCU), like a corporation for profit, has an obligation to contribute its fair share toward community funds that are used for diverse charitable, recreational, and educational needs of the public. The Administration views donations meeting this obligation as an activity incidental to a FCU's business within the scope of powers set forth in Section 107(15) of the Federal Credit Union Act. Consequently, FCU's may make contributions to the community organizations that are exempt from taxation pursuant to Section 501(c)(3) of the Internal Revenue Code.

Finally, FCU's should be aware of the following: that contributions, either direct or indirect, to candidates for a trade association or credit union league office do not fall within the scope of this interpretation; that FCU contributions and expenditures in connection with any election to any political office are prohibited by the Federal Election Campaign Act (2 U.S.C. 441b); that Article XIX, Section 4 of the Federal Credit Union Bylaws, concerning conflict of interest by officials and employees of an FCU, is applicable to the activities covered by this interpretation; and that, pursuant to Article VIII, Section 8 of the Federal Credit Union Bylaws, the minutes of the board of directors meeting at which any donation is authorized shall reflect both the amount and recipient of such donation.

A Federal credit union (FCU) may make contributions or donate funds to:

(1) An organization that is a tax-exempt organization under Section 501(c)(3) of the Internal Revenue Code, if such organization is located or conducts its activities in the community in which the FCU has a principal place of business;

(2) An organization that is a tax-exempt organization under Section 501(c)(3) of the Internal Revenue Code, if such organization operates primarily to promote and develop credit unions (including FCU's).

Any such contribution or donation must be approved by the FCU's board of directors, in such sum as the board deems to be in the best interest of the FCU, provided that such sum is sound given the financial condition of the FCU.

BIBLIOGRAPHY

Beyle, Thad L., ed. *State Government: CQ's Guide to Current Issues and Activities, 1996–97.* Washington, D.C.: Congressional Quarterly, 1996.

Hofman, Nancy Gendron. *How the U.S. Government Works.* Emeryville, CA: Ziff-Davis Press, 1995.

Moody, J. Caroll and Fite, Gilbert C. *The Credit Union Movement: Origins and Development 1850–1980.* Dubuque, IA: Kendall/Hunt Publishing, 1984.

Squire, Peverill; Lindsay, James M., Covington, Cary R., and Smith, Eric R.A.N. *Dynamics of Democracy.* Boston: McGraw-Hill, 1997.

U. S. Government. *The United States Government Manual 1997/98.* Washington, D.C.: Office of the Federal Register, National Archives and Records Service, General Services Administration, 1998.

Vote USA. *Democracy Owner's Manual.* Vote USA, 1995.

Witzeling, Ruth. *People, Not Profit: The Story of the Credit Union Movement.* Dubuque, IA: Kendall/Hunt Publishing, 1993.